## PRAISE FOR
### *WOODLAND PHILOSOPHY*

"No other living philosopher could have written this book. Sebastian Morello has produced a modern-day classic, a small miracle, really. *Woodland Philosophy* weaves together a deep philosophical account with an even deeper immersion in the truth, goodness, and beauty of the natural world, which earlier Christians often spoke of as God's other book of revelation. Morello writes movingly about the Creation, from which we've been disconnecting ourselves in the modern age. At the same time, he fearlessly defends the role of hunters and other true lovers of the woods and fields, currently maligned by our elites, who can open for us a path back to living well again, where we belong, in our proper home."
—**ROBERT ROYAL**, president of the Faith & Reason Institute and author of *The Martyrs of the New Millennium*

"Fieldsports, for Morello, are 'a kind of prayer.' Sebastian Morello provides a lucid, thrilling exploration of the intimate links between man the hunter, God, and the natural world. If you're only going to read one book about hunting, this is the one. It is also beautifully written, frequently witty, and refreshingly short."
—**CHARLIE PYE-SMITH**, author of *Rural Wrongs* and *Land of Plenty*

"Restoring us to what lives, breathes, suffers, and rises like steam against a backdrop of morning dew, Sebastian Morello's *Woodland Philosophy* is a paean to all that bleeds in the name of the Divine. Trekking a sure line between sentimentality and over-abstractionism, Morello offers a vision of the world that respects man's nature as cultivator and hunter as well as the challenges of 'nature's inner violence.'

Vivid, organic, and alive, *Woodland Philosophy* leads us through mushroom rings and shadowy groves to hallowed and dappled ground, ever aware of the wonder of Creation and our duties as its stewards."

—**NINA POWER**, author of *What Do Men Want?: Masculinity and Its Discontents*

"Sebastian Morello confronts the secular, technocratic, gnostic assumption that our highest good comes by way of emancipation from matter, indeed from the earth itself. His is a rare but vital voice exploring and explaining why our initiation into the countryside and all that that involves — especially, and provocatively, fieldsports — integrates us into the cycles of the cosmos and nurtures our capacity for belief and belonging."

—**GAVIN ASHENDEN**, Associate Editor of the *Catholic Herald*

"Sebastian Morello is fast becoming my favorite living conservative writer. *Woodland Philosophy* is a compelling call for a return to nature, where reality outfoxes the abstract. Nuanced, funny, well-traveled, broad-minded, and surgical, Morello crams into a paragraph what some writers would spin a whole book out of. This is a rare conservative who not only walks the talk but stalks the stags, in his freshly waxed Barbour coat."

—**TIM STANLEY**, Leader Writer at *The Telegraph*

# WOODLAND PHILOSOPHY

# WOODLAND PHILOSOPHY

## MEDITATIONS ON HUNTING, HIKING, AND HOLINESS

### SEBASTIAN MORELLO

*Foreword by Michael Martin*
*Afterword by Charles Coulombe*

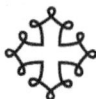

Angelico Press

For information, address:
Angelico Press, Ltd.
169 Monitor St.
Brooklyn, NY 11222
www.angelicopress.com

ppr 979-8-89280-156-0
cloth 979-8-89280-157-7
ebook 979-8-89280-158-4

Book and cover design
by Michael Schrauzer
Cover image:
"St Hubert's Vision,"
by William Morello

# CONTENTS

# AUTHOR'S NOTE ON BRITISH HUNTING TERMINOLOGY

AMERICANS AND BRITS HAVE DIFferent hunting terminology. As far as I understand, in the United States, hunting and fishing are distinguished, but beyond that, hunting quarry with hounds, shooting game birds with a shotgun, or pursuing deer with rifle or bow are all activities denoted by the word 'hunting.' In this, to my knowledge, Americans follow terminology which corresponds to that widely used by continental Europeans.

In the UK, 'hunting' means the following of a pack of hounds — either on horseback or on foot — which traditionally hunted fox, deer, hare, or mink (and during some periods, boar and otter). The killing with a shotgun of birds in flight — such as partridge, pheasant, or grouse — is called 'shooting.' The pursuit of animals with a rifle (bowhunting is illegal in the UK), such as deer or boar, is called 'stalking' — that is, unless the British sportsman in question happens to be pursuing an animal in Africa, where for some mysterious reason he opts for calling his sport 'hunting' rather than 'stalking.' And there are further categories; for example, the hunting of quarry with sighthounds such as greyhounds or lurchers has always been called 'coursing'; the waterside shooting of ducks and geese with a shotgun is called 'wildfowling.'

Moreover, hunting with hounds possesses its own lexicon that even most Brits can barely decipher. For example, the jackets worn by hunt staff and followers are always called 'coats.' A hound's tail is called a 'stern.' A fox's tail is called a 'brush.' Hounds don't bark but 'speak,' or if they are especially excited

then they're said to be in 'full cry.' The strange,
idiosyncratic jargon goes on and on.

Hunting with hounds was historically a central
part of British, especially English, culture. But there
are also venerable traditions of this sport throughout the European continent; it was outlawed in
Germany by Adolf Hitler, but it remains a very
important part of rural culture in France, where
chiefly stag, buck, boar, and hare are pursued. In
Britain, the hunting season for fox and hare lasts
almost half the year if you include autumn hunting in preparation for the Season proper, and then
serious addicts can join minkhound and staghound
packs through spring and summer. To this day,
it is normal for both country and town pubs to
have walls lined with hunting art and memorabilia,
testifying to the vital role hunting has played in
our culture.

Whilst hunting in general is a cherished part of
American culture, it often surprises sporting Brits
to learn that the American season for hunting deer
typically lasts only three or four months, depending
on the state. In the UK, whatever the time of year,
there is always a deer that can be stalked, with
one non-native species—the muntjac—having no
close season at all. Hence, passionate sportsmen are
accustomed in these isles to satiating their appetite
for *la chasse* all year round. In many ways, then, the
UK has been a sportsman's paradise, and it remains
something of a haven for fieldsporting activities
despite the constant interference of political med-
dlers and activists who continuously betray their
ignorance of rural life.

This 'note' is only to highlight that we Brits have
different hunting traditions both from our fellow
Europeans across the Channel and from our cousins
across the Pond, and this difference is reflected in

our use of distinct terminology. To spare the reader, whilst I sporadically deploy British hunting terminology, I have done my best to stick to a common and easily understandable vernacular throughout the text. And sometimes — where it has felt natural to do so — I have opted for 'hunting' as a generic term to denote all sporting activities traditionally entailing the pursuit of quarry, after the American fashion. I am confident that, despite the occasional appearance of British hunting terminology, or perhaps even partly because of it, sympathetic readers both from the US and from countries in continental Europe will enjoy the meditations herein.

"You will find more lessons in the woods than in books. Trees and stones will teach you what you cannot learn from masters."
— St Bernard of Clairvaux, *Letter 106*

"We rightly call philosophers 'hunters,' always panting away on the track of truth. Are they not, after all, hunting dogs? Socrates, in the *Republic*, says this is the perfect word for them.... Here, you wise dogs of the Academy; here, I am calling you for the chase."
— Marsilio Ficino, *De vita libri tres*

# HUNTING AND THE GIFT

THE FIRST FIREARM I EVER OWNED was a Harrington & Richardson, Topper Model 158 .410 shotgun that I received from my parents as a Christmas gift when I was eight years old. Though I was not small for my age, I was small enough that my father needed to saw off some of the buttstock so I could reach the trigger with the gun firmly shouldered. A single-shot, break-action model, I still have it and use it mostly to hunt rabbits on and around my farm in Michigan. It is a storehouse of memory and wonder.

Guns and hunting run deep in the historical imagination of my family. My father descended from French voyageurs on his father's side, men who came to the New World in the eighteenth century to seek their fortunes by hunting and trapping with a freedom unknown to them in their country of origin, where hunting was a luxury reserved for the nobility. They were also men who intermarried with Native women, which connected them biologically to this land and imparted a two-fold legacy to their descendants, who upheld the tradition of hunting and a reverence for the wild over the course of centuries. My father, a true heir, was an incredible marksman and even as a ten-year-old boy was a champion skeet shooter who could routinely take out two clay pigeons with one shot as they crossed before him on the range.

With this heritage, it is no surprise that all of my cousins on the Martin side hunt, and whenever we get together the conversation almost immediately

falls to hunting—even at funerals. Like our Catholic
faith, it is an intrinsic part of our cultural identity,
going back to earliest childhood. Indeed, some of my
fondest childhood memories are those of my father
coming home from the field and helping him dress
ducks or squirrels or rabbits, and then watching
him clean his guns over newspaper spread across
the basement floor, enjoying the smell of blood
mixed with gunpowder and tobacco. To this day, the
scent of Hoppe's No. 9 Gun Bore Cleaner remains
a powerful and magical intoxicant that evokes in
me a desire to take to the woods and fields.

   In addition to the social and cultural aspects
of my hunting life, there has also simultaneously
existed a haunting spiritual dimension to it. Part of
this, no doubt, has to do with an answer my father
gave to one of my first theological inquiries: "Dad,
what's heaven like?" To which he answered: "Like
hunting. It's like hunting." That sounded reasonable
enough. Though I can make no claims as to what
heaven is really like, I do know that my time in
the woods has often bordered on the mystical. One
November morning, for example, a buck presented
itself to me through a light fog as it emerged from
a swale, first the shadow of the antlers, and eventually his magnificent head and white breast. But
it was not as if I had hunted *him*; it was as though
he had given himself to *me*. As Robert Kelly writes
in his prose poem, "The Heavenly Country":

> At night it was almost cold, so we sleep with
> blankets or walked out in sweaters early
> morning to see deer or whatever else might
> reveal itself to us. That it is a matter of It
> willing to reveal to Us I have never doubted.[1]

---

[1] Robert Kelly, *The Convections* (Santa Barbara: Black Sparrow
Press, 1978), 63.

There is something about participation in the rhythms and works of the Creation that inspires intuitions that are unmistakably spiritual in nature; for it is there that one can, on occasion, discover the Wild of God.

The legends and tales of hunters and the hunt are replete with depictions of an unwary hunter wandering into an Otherworld. *Carmina Gadelica*, the Scottish folklorist Alexander Carmichael's astonishing collection of Highland charms, prayers, and lore includes three versions of the tale "The Hunter and the Fairy." The stories tell of a hunter, having left his beloved milkmaid at home, seeking his quarry through wood and field when he stumbles upon a fairy. The fairy then falls in love with the hunter; but after he rejects her advances, she curses his beloved:

> But thou man who rangest rough grounds,
> And hast banished my comely looks,
> My hope fell altogether from me
> At seeing thee in the fairy hill.
>
> . . .
>
> But thou man who rangest yonder,
> Bear a farewell from me and tell it,
> Bear word unto the dairymaid
> That I am she who has condemned her.[2]

Danger inhabits the wilds that lead to the Otherworld, but these are dangers always already present to all those who hunt. Indeed, the fairytales tell of metaphysical danger, not of the eternal damnation variety, but of the kind that reminds those of us who participate in the wild that we belong to two different orders of reality, whose claims upon us

---

[2] "The hunter and the fairy" in Alexander Carmichael, *Carmina Gadelica: Hymns and Incantations Collected in the Highlands and Islands of Scotland in the Last Century*, ed. C. J. Moore (Hudson, NY: Lindisfarne Press, 1992), 506, 481.

often come into conflict. Thus, we find ourselves enmeshed in the ever-present aporia of being.

Sebastian Morello is mindful of both the dangers and the vicissitudes inherent in entering the Wild of God. As he writes in these pages, following Tennyson, nature is "red in tooth and claw." Nature is the realm of demonic figures such as Herne the Hunter and Jarylo, but it is also the realm of divine revelation, as seen in the legends of Saints Eustace and Hubert. This world is fallen, but not *only* fallen. Indeed, I believe that what we have in these two different responses to the Wild of God is what the German mystical writer Jacob Boehme, inspired by the Rhineland mystics, describes as the World of God's Wrath and the World of God's Love. These two 'worlds' are inseparable from each other because they are one. Indeed, for Boehme, our world is a meeting of the Realm of Light and the Realm of Darkness and Fire. Together they are what the great Russian polymath and mystic Pavel Florensky would call an antinomy by which "the statics and the dynamics of the rational mind exclude one another, although they cannot exist without one another."[3] As William Blake concludes his "Auguries of Innocence":

> God Appears & God is Light
>> To those poor souls who dwell in Night
>> But does a Human Form Display
>> To those who Dwell in Realms of Day.[4]

Of course, God's love is never changing, but the warmth of His love must contend with a Creation

---

[3] See his *The Pillar and Ground of the Truth: An Essay in Orthodox Theodicy in Twelve Letters,* trans. Boris Jakim (Princeton: Princeton University Press, 1997), 345.
[4] *The Complete Poetry and Prose of William Blake,* ed. David V. Erdman, rev. ed. (Berkeley: University of California Press, 1982), lines 129–32.

Hunting and the Gift

in rebellion, and hence His love often feels like consuming fire to those in the throes of their fallenness and insulated from the sophianic splendour that is the Glory of the Lord. This duality—and its very real dangers—is a feature of the Creation itself, in fact beautifully illustrated by the mushroom kingdom about which Morello so insightfully writes: "Hunting mushrooms is very dangerous. Whereas the hunting of most quarry entails danger only for the one hunted, many mushrooms will take their predators down with them." Even psychedelic mushrooms, which a psychotherapist friend of mine calls "an antidote for atheism," can invoke both the oceanic feeling of oneness with the cosmos and unmitigated terror. If God doesn't find you by way of the first effect, he might find you via the second.

To be honest, books on hunting by intellectuals the caliber of Sebastian Morello are few and far between; and current cultural conditions, certainly among the ruling intelligentsia, are openly hostile to the mode of being Morello proposes here. Nevertheless, the intellectual life alienated from the Book of Nature is not a life worth living and, in the end, detrimental to human flourishing. As Morello writes, "The intellectual who is not an outdoorsman is too great a threat to his fellow man, whom he will no doubt eventually come to plague with his ideas." The intellectual life, lacking immersion in the Wild of God, has very little to offer on its own, which is why inevitably it deposits in stagnation and cynicism. What the Wild offers, as Morello shows throughout these pages, is the absolute gratuitousness of God revealed through Creation: that the world, despite its ferocity, is always *Gift*. This book, echoing that great bestowal, proves likewise a rich engagement in the mystery of All That Is.

Michael Martin
*Stella Matutina Farm*

# INTRODUCTION

IN THE AUTUMN OF 2022, AT THE invitation of Roger Scruton's widow, Sophie, I delivered a lecture to members of the Roger Scruton Legacy Foundation on the lasting importance of her late husband's 1998 book *On Hunting*, a masterpiece of agrestic apologetics. The response I received to that lecture was very encouraging, planting in my mind the idea for this volume. The meditations that comprise this book spring from my love of hunting and of the outdoors in general. Ever since I was a small child, being outdoors has been a constant source of inspiration for me. From the panorama of a rural landscape down to the fine veins that run through a sycamore leaf, the outdoors has disclosed to me the hidden animating force of the cosmos, creation's 'Secret Fire,' as Gandalf the Grey put it during his confrontation with the Balrog.

I have travelled through Africa, Asia, and much of Europe. I have trekked to the top of great mountains such as Mount Kenya, crossed over the Dolomites, scaled the crags of the Himalayan Langtang region, and rambled up lesser peaks like Snowdon in Wales. I have camped out under the stars on the savanna, to be awoken at midnight by the growling of lions; I have slept in temples dedicated to the devastating power of Shiva; I have wandered in pilgrimage to the Virgin's surviving shrines, hidden in an otherwise apostatised Europe. These days, though, I work as an academic, writer, and frequently a public speaker, which all entails a great deal of my time taken up with typing away at my desk. Yet each day, in the morning and the afternoon, the computer is put to sleep and out into the woodlands or fields I hike with my dog. Then, God's magical voice speaks in His emanated creation, the deceptive domain of intellectual idea-play is banished, and reality floods my soul in these eremitical ramblings.

I love to walk — whether a full day's hike or a morning stroll — but walking lends itself to an apprehension of the world from the perspective of a spectator or observer. Apprehension from the perspective of participation, which is quite different — and a mode of attention whose importance I reflect upon recurrently throughout these meditations — I found in hunting. When hunting, it is not only the magical voice of God that is heard, but in entering the natural drama of death and regeneration, the hunter — oneself — speaks back in the very same divine language. Thus, for me, fieldsports are a kind of prayer, and I've learned that such a view isn't unique to me, which may explain why everywhere except in the spiritually asphyxiated lands of the United Kingdom, sporting pursuits remain connected with ancient traditions, rituals, liturgies, and blessings.

Various conversations with Roger Scruton (to whom this book is dedicated) during his research supervision of my MA and PhD taught me not only that fieldsports and outdoorsmanship can be worthy objects of philosophical reflection, but that they might build a foundation for such reflection in general. Indeed, for those strange, philosophically-inclined people who also love the outdoors, there are few moments that lead to such contemplative depths as those found amid fieldsporting pursuits.

Of course, like any human history, the history of hunting is a chequered one. In the United States, the white tail deer was almost hunted out of existence, and yet it was also the hunting community that established the various conservation organisations for its protection, bringing the species back to

astonishing numbers. It was hunters who pushed
for legally recognised hunting seasons to protect
the white tail deer from the hunting community's
less scrupulous members. And it is largely due to
the responsible sportsmanship of ethical hunters in
Africa that many of that continent's most majestic
mammals have not had their habitats completely
destroyed by urban sprawl and industrialised agriculture, or been killed to the point of eradication
by the scourge of poaching.

This book is not solely about hunting; it is about
loving the outdoors and the connection of that love
to a particular worldview. It is important, though,
to address the role of hunting from the outset, on
account of the controversies that surround this
most natural of activities. Beyond the importance
of outdoorsmanship for the life of the mind and
for the conserving of culture—which I think are
paramount considerations—there are very serious
practical aspects to hunting that ought not to be
neglected. Once a species ceases to stand among
the respected quarry of a country, it is inevitably
reduced to a mere agricultural pest. This is what
has happened in Kenya, which banned hunting in
1977 and has since seen a 70 percent reduction of
its wildlife. The opposite happened in South Africa,
which, for example, successfully saved the white
rhino from extinction through its conservation-
based hunting industry. It's not just Africa that has
such a story to tell. In England, the great red deer
herds of the west country were treated as pests until
staghound packs were established in the nineteenth
century that actively protected the deer and managed their health via hunting old and sick members
of the herd. So too, roe deer were nearly extirpated
until the emergence of continental-style stalking in
the 1950s that elevated them to a treasured game

animal—consequently they are now flourishing throughout the land. The fox and the hare were protected by rural communities as a quarry species until Prime Minister Tony Blair's 2004 outlawing of hunting with hounds, after which it has been open season all year round, during which these creatures are shot with firearms. Now, these wonderful animals have disappeared entirely from some areas of the British Isles. My point is a basic one that history has repeatedly verified: in places populated by humans, fieldsports and conservation are correlated.

I remain unconvinced that anti-hunting sentiment has ever been about animal welfare or the minimising of animal suffering. For example, in Britain, a study carried out in the mid-1990s estimated that domestic cats, whose numbers were at around 9 million, killed 88 million birds and 164 million small mammals annually. This same study found that among all activities investigated as reasons for the killing of wild animals, hunting and shooting were responsible for just 6.006 percent of deaths, whereas cats accounted for 82 percent. A later study, carried out in 2022, revealed that domestic cats annually killed between 160–270 million wild animals, around a quarter of which were birds. In early 2025, a report entitled "Responsible ownership and care of domestic cats in Scotland,"[1] published by the Scottish Animal Welfare Committee, publicised research which noted that the "number of wild prey killed [by cats] could reach at least 700 million vertebrates per year in the UK."[2]

---

[1] https://www.gov.scot/publications/report-responsible-ownership-care-domestic-cats-felis-catus-scotland/pages/9/.

[2] Tim Bonner, CEO of the Countryside Alliance, wrote an interesting commentary on the above referenced Report: https://www.countryside-alliance.org/features/tim-bonner-should-cats-be-banned?.

Domestic cats are thus a very serious problem from a conservationist perspective, given that the UK has a rapidly declining population of songbirds and wild mammals. (Moreover, cats kill in such a famously slow and torturous way that they are frequently selected as model animals for studies of acute aggression in predators.) As is revealed by the above examples of research into the adverse effects of cats, as time passes the feline problem is escalating and intensifying. It is no exaggeration to say that the domestic cat is an ecological disaster of great magnitude. Yet, no one has called for the banning of cat ownership—despite the extraordinary dev-astation cats cause to wildlife and the cruelty they deploy whilst doing it.[3]

Due to the ecological challenges posed by cats, not to mention those presented by urbanisation and the habitat destruction caused by industrial agricul-ture—none of which seems to attract the adverse attention that hunting receives—it is difficult not to conclude that anti-hunting attitudes are not at root concerned with the good of animals but with the emotional lives of those who hunt. Anti-hunting people think that only a despicable monster would hunt a wild animal, and hence it is normal for anti-hunting people to use de-humanising language like 'scum' and related words to denote fieldsporting men and women. But as I argue in Chapter 3, entitled "The Wild Hunt," if I am correct in my analysis of the basis for which anti-hunting sentiment exists, then the anti-hunting lobby is correct in their iden-tification of the core issue. Let me explain. Animals suffer and they cause suffering to other animals,

---

[3] A helpful overview of the two earlier studies can be found in Charlie Pye-Smith's excellent work of investigative journalism, *Rural Wrongs: Hunting and the Unintended Consequences of Bad Law* (Frome: The R.S. Surtees Society, 2023), 64-68.

and they always will—that is a fact. The question, then, is not whether we can prevent that suffering, but whether our direct involvement in the realm of animal suffering makes *us* more cruel. If it necessarily does, then we ought to ban hunting, just as we banned bear-baiting and other obvious expressions of human cruelty. But if hunting is different, and it does *not* make us more cruel, at least in principle, then we ought no longer to worry about the emotional lives of field sportsmen. Instead, we ought to resituate the discussion of hunting on the two *real* issues: 1) wildlife and habitat conservation and 2) the role of fieldsports in human culture—which are the two aspects of hunting that responsible and ethical hunters have always chiefly cared about. It may turn out that the not uncommon hatred towards hunters and the comparative disinterest in the plight of battery-farmed animals were together the real indicator of where our culture's cruelty lay when it came to animals.

My view is that the controversies that orbit outdoorsmanship and fieldcraft—at the heart of which will always be hunting, shooting, stalking, and fishing—are not merely about whether we're compassionate towards animals. Rather, those controversies are part of a much deeper 'culture war.' The trouble is that neither the anti-hunting lobby nor the fieldsports communities seem fully to grasp this. Were the anti-hunting lobby really concerned with animal welfare, they would have carried out at least elementary research into whether Blair's "Hunting Act 2004" has improved the condition and quality of life both for traditional quarry species and other animals around Britain. But no such investigation by the anti-hunting lobby has been carried out, despite its massive financial resources. Charlie Pye-Smith's *Rural Wrongs*, a work of investigative

journalism that presents the effects of the Hunting
Act on British wildlife, reveals that the effects of
the Act have been disastrous for the animals with
which we share the countryside.

Before the Hunting Act 2004, The Countryside Alliance, a charity, staged one of the largest
demonstrations ever held in London. That city's
inhabitants watched with amazement as 400,000
people formed a river of tweed and waxed cotton
that meandered through the capital in defence of
hunting. The question of whether to outlaw hunting
with hounds occupied 240 hours of Parliamentary
time, whereas the decision by the same government to invade Iraq took 18 hours. This is clearly
a 'culture war.'

The fact is that ever since the so-called Enlightenment, there has been an ongoing debate plaguing
the Occident concerning what man *is* and what he
ought to become. Does man come to a state of flourishing by emancipating himself from his history,
his identity, his nationality, and—through technology—his embodied existence and union with the
earth, in order to enter some liberated condition of
the pre-social 'authentic self'? Or does man flourish
by a process of being inducted deep into his history,
his sense of place and community, and ultimately
into the cycle of the cosmos of which he is a part?
The degree of sympathy you have for fieldsports
will largely depend on how you answer.

People who hunt often say that there are important cultural aspects to hunting that shouldn't be
neglected, like the localistic culture-fostering and
community-building that hunting served to support down the centuries. But what people do not
realise when they make such arguments is that *that*
is precisely the aspect of hunting that many of its
opponents hate so much. After all, when Prime

Minister Tony Blair banned hunting with hounds two decades ago, he was at the time embarking on a very comprehensive project of sweeping away what was left of merry old England, and creating a new, utopian, classless, purely meritocratic, globalist country, whose future was going to be forged in the dual-furnace of hawkish war-waging alongside the United States and ongoing bureaucratic integration with the EU. Attachment to kin and place, of the kind that hunting so inconveniently generates, was deemed by our modern managerial elites to be exactly what would hold Britain back.

A major theme of these meditations is my concern that both the ideologies of modernity and the new technologies with which we're all having to contend, are sundering us from the actual world and relocating us in a virtual world. There, in that synthetic realm of our own making, we are beginning to be re-created as spectral instances of opinion-generating bots — rather than the irreplaceable and accountable *persons* that we discover ourselves to be when settled in real places and inducted into real communities.

For centuries, there has been a mounting tension between those whose assumptions about the world are based on a mechanistic metaphor on the one hand and those who opt for an organicist metaphor on the other. Where one sees the place of man in the world will largely depend on which metaphor one's assumptions presuppose. I am resolutely an organicist and I believe that the mechanistic metaphor that had its ascendency in the Enlightenment and has stricken us ever since, has slowly disintegrated our minds and in turn unravelled our culture. We can't even contribute to culture anymore, let alone establish a culture, and this is because we don't know how to civilisationally cultivate, for cultivation is an organic activity. It's not

clear to me how we escape from the rut in which
this process has stuck us, but I firmly believe that
the woodlands, the fields, the rivers, and all the
animals with which we share them, can teach us
a great deal.

The reader will detect—for it is hardly well-
hidden—that my love of the outdoors is inextricably
linked to a wider religious and philosophical worldview, which I attempt to disclose in a dispersed way
throughout these meditations. It is my conviction
that the ancient Greeks were correct to centre the
pursuit of human flourishing on three foundational
institutions: the academy, the gymnasium, and the
temple. All three institutions find a special syn-
thesis in outdoorsmanship, in which one's knowledge of the world and practical wisdom become
embodied in movement and activity, unavoidably
leading—at least, in my experience—to adoration
of the world's Creator.

# ACKNOWLEDGEMENTS

FIRST, MY DEEPEST THANKS GOES TO my wife, who is an untypically tolerant vegetarian. Thanks also to my children; observing their love of the outdoors develop—unfolding in hiking, foraging, hunting, and horse riding—has been without any doubt among the greatest joys of my life. They love to be out in the woods or in the fields, and through their eyes I daily rediscover the wonder that is right and just before God's creation. I also thank my parents, who wisely gifted to me an air rifle and a spaniel when I was a child, thereby securing my profound affection for the English countryside in the decades that have followed.

I thank the committee, hunt staff, and members of the Old Berkeley Beagles, with whom it has been wonderful to follow hounds over the years, and whom it has been an honour to serve as whipper-in, committee member, and finally as a Master of Hounds. A very special thanks goes to my friend Declan Jones, who trained me to stalk deer with a centrefire rifle in exchange for tutorials in metaphysics. And I am immensely grateful to William Maitland-Makgill-Crichton who, in guiding me through the wilderness of South Africa's Great Karoo in pursuit of kudu and wildebeest, taught me that in this stifling, overly technologized epoch, it is nonetheless still possible to enjoy that wonderful experience that I feared had vanished from our world: an adventure.

I thank Charlie Pye-Smith and Jim Barrington for their excellent work to encourage a better understanding of hunting, animal welfare, and conservation—it has been a joy to work with them both.

Mario and Ellen Fantini have my profoundest thanks; it is in their outstanding journal, *The*

*European Conservative*, that the meditations which later became the chapters of this volume first appeared. My thanks to my brother, William Morello, for his beautiful watercolour painting of Saint Hubert's vision that he produced for this book's cover. Michael Martin's Foreword provides the reader with the perfect initiation into the spirit of this book, and I'm grateful to him for writing it; his own work has been an important source of inspiration for me. And I thank Charles Coulombe for his Afterword, which offers an excellent coda on which to end, revealing that between the fieldcraft of the hunter and the prudential governing of the statesman there is a certain harmony of which modern politicians would be wise to take note. Finally, my thanks to John Riess and the staff at Angelico Press for publishing this work.

# 1

# THE PROBLEM OF
# AN URBAN ESCHATON

THE SCREECH OF THE RAIL TRACK underneath the train reached an almost eardrum-piercing volume. The carriage rocked from side to side. Every face was glued to a phone screen. Some passengers—considerately—used headphones, but most of them just let their devices blare out a tinny and irritating noise, filling the carriage with a jarring mix of TikTok videos, trashy sitcom episodes, and rap music. It was a barbarian spectacle. Women with half their hair shaved off. Sunken-eyed and unmuscular men with black nail varnish. Sharp bits of metal protruding out of every face. Ripped up jeans. Noses with bull-rings. Mutilated, stretched ears. Blue hair. Green hair. Tattooed hands. Tattooed arms. Tattooed legs. Tattooed necks. Tattooed faces. Clothes tight where they shouldn't be; loose where they should be fitted. Everything warped, and twisted, and wounded, and distorted. Pale, hopeless faces, occasionally presenting a pitiable imitation of joy with each excitement provided by the little device in their hands—a parasite that governs every moment of recreation when modern people momentarily cease to be cogs in the machine and become underground zombies instead. This is a vision of hell. This is modern London.

I lived in London for some years. Not a bad part of London. I lived in Notting Hill, in a nice house in which I rented a large room. In fact, the building once belonged to Cardinal Manning, and

I used to sip ruby port from the old churchman's
crystal glasses whilst smoking roll-up cigarettes
under the gothic arch of my bedroom window.
Despite my privileged dwellings and the romantic
persona I successfully cultivated for myself there, I
was haunted by the desire to get out. Every Friday
evening, I hopped into my hatchback and fled to
my family home in the countryside, and wouldn't
return until early on Monday morning, arriving
just in time at the publishing house where I worked.

Beyond its landmarks, most parts of London
look like any other part. I suppose it's not as bad as
former communist metropolises, but it's not much
better. London is a kind of Lockean hell. That is, it
exemplifies the atomic anthropology of John Locke:
a concrete jungle in which everyone subsists as an
isolated individual pursuing his or her own private interests. London is a reversal of the ideal of
the Grecian *polis*, which entails a people organically
emerging together, pursuing the common end of
human flourishing.

The very appearance of most Londoners testifies to
their desire to be estranged from one another. People
used to dress nicely for the sake of manners. For
men, a lapelled jacket, collared shirt, ironed trousers,
and leather shoes, were a way of saying to anyone
they met, "I have made an effort." In contrast, the
untidy hairdos, facial mutilations, and ripped up
clothes of our contemporary urban dwellers signify
a massive 'piss off' to everyone who looks upon the
gloominess that they embody. They are in pursuit
of radical individualism and self-realisation, and
consequently have become mere solipsistic autom-
atons—blobs of grey that are interchangeable with
any of the city's ten million 'radical individuals.'

As I looked around the underground train carriage, and meditated on this exhibition of human

misery, it occurred to me that the appropriate emotional response would be that of rage. Everything about this vision conveyed an absence of manners and decency. I ought to be offended, I reasoned. I suppose I *am* offended, I concluded. But I didn't really feel it, since I had become well anaesthetised, over years of working in London, to the infernal character of the place.

My escape from London coincided with my marriage and subsequent arrival of our first child, to whom we gave a home beyond the Chiltern Hills, on the fringe of England's Home Counties. Now out of the city, I re-waxed my old Barbour coat. I started hunting through the Season, learned how to forage, and I bought an estate car, a whippet, and a fine pair of gumboots. I learned the names of the trees, birds, and other animals, and I got to know farmers and the surrounding community. I rediscovered the God who resides not in the Temple alone, but the God of the eighth Psalm — the God of the outdoors. I embraced the countryside with an enthusiasm unknown to me in my childhood, when I didn't know anything *but* the countryside. Here among the fields, hedgerows, and copses, I found — and continue to find — a source of solace which was inaccessible in the city, a solace I enjoyed as a child, and which I had come to taste only in fleeting escapes on weekends.

As a believer in the Christian religion, it disturbs me that heaven is presented to us in Holy Scripture as a distinctly metropolitan experience. In the twentieth chapter of the Book of the Apocalypse, shortly after the doom of Satan, the dead are raised from their slumber and brought before the Judgement Seat. The wicked are then cast into the Lake of Fire and a vision is presented of the habitation that awaits the blessed:

> I saw the holy city, New Jerusalem, coming
> down out of heaven from God, made ready
> as a bride adorned for her husband. And I
> heard a loud voice from the throne saying,
> "Behold the dwelling of God and men, and
> he will dwell with them. And they will be
> his people, and God himself will be with
> them as their God." (Apocalypse 21:2-3)

The book then goes on to describe the celestial city, its size, what materials it is made from, and where the Temple is situated within its walls. Make no mistake, Holy Writ is clear: if you're saved by God's grace, then you're in for an urban eternity. And yet it is from urban life that I fled. I venture into London only out of necessity now, a few times a year at most, and make a point of sulking for the duration of my visits.

Of course, I draw consolation from the fact that it was a rustic life the Lord Jesus Christ knew when he was personally present among us, growing up in a rural village (Nazareth is believed to have had a population of between 500 and 1,500 people). He spent much time up in the hills, out on the water, or walking in the fields and talking to simple people. From among those who worshipped Him as a baby, some were angels and some were Persian priests of a foreign religion, but among His own people of Israel only the shepherds of the hills prostrated before Him. His metaphors were largely agricultural and pastoral. He made short visits to towns, but note that His visits to Jerusalem were marked by His separation from His parents, His exhibition of righteous rage in the Temple, and finally His torture and death. And yet, in the Apocalypse, when the angel takes John the Divine into the countryside, it is only to better view the New Jerusalem which is his true home.

No doubt my notion of the New Jerusalem should not be wholly conditioned by my experience of London (though William Blake dreamt that the former might be instantiated in the locale of the latter). Cities were once very different to what they are today. Indeed, cities used to give the impression that their inhabitants were gathered for a common purpose, not for mere private pursuits. The European city, certainly, used to resemble more the Grecian ideal, so admired by the thinkers and patrons of the Renaissance. Every city, for example, had three things: a cathedral, a square, and a hall. These three features indicated the desired unity of the people who lived there together.

The ancient market town in whose outskirts we live is still marked by these three features. It is dominated by the church's 190-foot spire (adorned by great stone angels gifted to the parish by Geoffrey Chaucer's granddaughter, the Countess of Suffolk). At the town's heart is the square, whose centre has a market cross—a beautiful monument encircled with medieval statues of bearded bishops. Twice a week, the market appears (which received its charter twenty years after the Norman conquest), during which townsfolk gather to buy cheeses, baked goods, flowers, and pigs' ears for their dogs. Up on the hill is the town hall, which is no longer a gathering place for people to work out their disputes and call upon local government, but you can still get in touch with officials there to deal with problems without too much inconvenience. Our nearby town is a little version of what is found on a larger scale throughout Europe, at Siena, Ghent, Narbonne, Amsterdam, Salzburg, Brasov, Cambridge, Nice, and elsewhere.

The distinction between town and country was not always so sharp. At the beginning of the *Phaedrus*, Socrates and the man after whom the dialogue is

named meet in the heart of Athens, presumably at
the parent of all public squares, the Agora. Within
minutes, however, they are out in the countryside,
where they find the proper setting to discuss love
and madness, and more importantly, to pray together.
Some cities remain that continue to blur the distinction between the urban and the rural, and they are
the most cherished cities — there are few places in
Florence, for example, where the Tuscan hills cannot be seen. Florence would not be Florence if that
weren't so, and part of that city's breathtaking beauty
is accounted for by this very feature (Savonarola
may be forgiven, I think, for believing that Florence
would be the location of the New Jerusalem). There
are still towns and small cities in England where a
tweed jacket and corduroys do not look out of place.

Whilst escape from the city for the sake of prayer
and meditation is a recurring motif of Western literature, and one that played an important role in the
life of Jesus Christ, one of the great achievements of
Western civilisation has been that of sanctifying the
city. I am told that Oxford, once a training centre
for clerics, evolved with the Eucharist in mind. The
roads and buildings were situated so as to allow for
Oxford's inhabitants to get to a tabernacle in the
shortest possible time, that 'ocular communions'
(worship of the sacred host during its elevation at
Holy Mass) could be made in between tutorials. The
layout of Oxford still testifies to its pious history,
apparently. Throughout Europe, cities often emerged
in the shadow of some great monastery, so that the
monks could sanctify the world of trade as they
had sanctified the land on which trade depended.

But over the centuries, our cities apostatised.

As the cities ceased to view trade as a means,
and began to see it as an end, making cash and
commodities the gods of the metropolitan arena,

countryside people frequently held out, continuing to build their shrines to the Living God. One by one, as rural people generally remained faithful, cities formally disavowed God, demanding that He keep to the country and out of their business. It was largely the farming families of sixteenth-century England who remained loyal to the Roman Catholic religion. In the West Country, priests who abandoned the ancient faith were found in pieces, having been chopped up by zealous farmers who had found new uses for their agricultural tools. Thereafter, as people compromised, Church establishment in England was nonetheless upheld by the rural squirearchy and countryfolk as the cities and towns became hotbeds of religious dissent and puritan sectarianism (the fast road to secularism, as John Henry New- man famously argued in his 1879 *Biglietto Speech*). The eighteenth century had seen France's farmers in the Vendée, Maine, and Brittany refuse to go along with the secularisation of the 'Church's eldest daughter.' The following century, the countryside people of Tyrol rejected the tide of secularism and marched under the banner of the Sacred Heart.

I wonder if, in the Christian vision of history as a "long defeat" containing only "some samples or glimpses of final victory," as Tolkien put it, the apostasy of the cities is meant to be providentially didactic.[1] Certainly, Europe's pre-modern cities are magnificent enough to teach us that the *polis* is our true home, and union with one another our proper condition. Cities, however, have since become rotten enough to suggest that no earthly city can be our true home, and that union with one another in this life is always enjoyed on a knife-edge.

---

[1] Humphrey Carpenter and Christopher Tolkien, eds., *The Letters of J.R.R. Tolkien* (London: HarperCollins, 1995), Letter #195, 255.

Perhaps, like the distant city in a Flemish master's landscape, in this fallen world our urban home must always be an ideal in the background which cannot be located anywhere here below. Like the sign of peace given to Noah, were you to approach it, it would only keep retreating.

It occurs to me, however, that for the Christian it is possible to consider the city more positively, namely as mission territory. Certainly, it is clear from the Augustinian doctrine that the baptised are called to leave the City of Man and enter the City of God, and the faithful who live in earthly cities are no less called. It is plausible, in fact, that the city-dweller must interiorly enter the City of God precisely so as to exteriorly incarnate it in the earthly city. If so, I can only imagine that this requires herculean spiritual strength, which I certainly did not possess. No, it was clear that I would not conquer the city—it would conquer me. In turn, perhaps I chose the lesser part, and fled the city for the minor mission of carving out and redeeming a little part of the world which would so willingly give itself to my apostolate.

## 2

# BETWEEN THE DEER AND THE IDEA

FOR A WHILE, I WAS TORMENTED by sporadic insomnia. One night, I lay in bed staring up at the ceiling as my mind raced with a hundred new ideas. It was not the first time that this had happened.

I drew back the curtain and held up my wristwatch to the full moon's light; it was 3:00 a.m. I went to my study, where I jotted down a few thoughts on a notepad in the hope that their transference into an extramental condition would free me from them. No dice. I returned to bed and lay there for another hour. It was no use.

By 4:20 a.m., I was downstairs and drinking coffee. I suddenly realised what I needed: I needed the woods. I put on my jacket and walking boots, woke up the dog, and got into the car. By 4:45 a.m. I was in the heart of the Chiltern Hills, hiking deep into the woods. I have always loved these woods. As a teenager, I would drive my little car out there and walk to find my favourite tree, an ancient and somewhat deformed elm that I named Agatha. In those years, sitting in this tree's branches, I read Sun Tzu's *The Art of War* and the *Bhagavad Gita*, and undertook what turned out to be a life-changing reading of the Gospel of St John.

Many years ago, during one of my intimate moments with Agatha, I heard the gentle rustling of cloven hooves below. Rummaging beneath me, as I lay out on one of Agatha's thick branches, was a large herd of fallow deer. I never moved a muscle, and they never saw me. For perhaps five minutes, suspended a few feet above their heads, I watched them. I enjoyed a similar experience by a lake some years later, staying in Nepal's Chitwan rainforest, when a rhinoceros stepped out of the forest and, taking no notice of me, bathed before me for nearly an hour. There was something especially remarkable, however, about my encounter with the fallow herd that day. Many times since, I have returned to watch the deer in that wood, and the novelty of seeing them has never worn off.

Often, as a youngster, when I was researching for my college diploma, I would find a spot outdoors to do so. Even now, after hours in my study, my habit is to take my dog into the countryside and wander about, inspecting the trees, looking for wildlife, or collecting nettles for soup. There is sense to this behaviour. The life of the mind is fundamentally dangerous when divorced from the world. Indeed, intellectuals have a moral duty to seek out ways of encountering reality—the thing out there—if they are to avoid becoming a tremendous nuisance to others, a trait so common among their kind.

Why does the life of the mind often become disconnected from reality? The answer, I think, may be found in the problematic composition of reality itself.

Philosophy began not with questions about isolated emotional states, or personal identity, or the limits of knowledge, but with the question of the stuff around us. The pre-Socratics, for example, focused on finding some single principle that would account for the world's existence. Plato, with his theory of the 'perfect forms,' was undertaking the same task, as was Aristotle with his famous account of the 'four causes.' And philosophy continued on in this way.

For this reason, philosophy was generally taught along the lines of the following curriculum: philosophy of nature (what *is* all the stuff out there?), metaphysics (what *accounts* for the stuff out there?), epistemology (how do *I know* about the stuff out there?), philosophical anthropology (*what am I*, this thing asking these questions?), ethics (knowing what I know, *how should I live?*) and politics (knowing what *we* know, *how should we live together?*). These are all questions of *being*: what is *being* and what is it *to be?* Somewhere along the way, however, *being* dropped out of philosophy.

In response to people like me who complain about the disappearance of fundamental philosophical questions from the discipline of philosophy, it is often said that scientific investigation and experimentation have replaced philosophical questions of *being*. This, however, is clearly false, since the scientific enterprise presupposes all sorts of philosophical conclusions about the inherent intelligibility of the universe that science aims at exploring, as well as the capacity of the human mind to grasp that intelligibility. How, then, did *being* drop out of philosophy?

Again, it seems to me that the problem lies with the inherently problematic composition of reality itself. Let me explain. All that is, *is*. That is to say: everything that has being, exists. Hopefully we can all agree on that. But everything that exists also exists as *something*. If you see a large tawny object moving through the woods, you know that something is there, an existent being of some sort, but only when you have identified it as a deer do you know *what* it is. In turn, everything that *is* is composed of two principles: existence and essence. Everything that *is* also *is as something* (indeed, these correspond to the existential and predicative forms of the copula 'is,' but we needn't worry about that).

The question arises, is the distinction between *existence* and *essence* merely a distinction of the mind, or are the things out there in the world really such compositions of two knowable principles? Classically—and it is certainly the answer that makes the most sense to me—thinkers have argued that the distinction between existence and essence is not merely a mental (or *logical*) distinction but a *real* distinction. First, *that* something exists does not explain why it exists as *this* kind of thing, since other things also exist which are different kinds of things. Second, this kind of thing need not have ever existed; for example, any given deer, or all deer, might conceivably have never come into being. In turn, the essence of a thing does not explain why it exists. Indeed, it is perfectly possible to conceive of essences that are not conjoined to any corresponding principle of existence—just think of any mythical creature. So, it seems that these principles are *real*, rather than merely mental categories, for *existence* and *essence* explain the being of any given thing and are simultaneously irreducible to each other.

So far, so good. I call this composition of reality 'problematic,' however, because it can all get rather messy when a mind turns up. The human mind knows *what* something is—a fallow deer, say—because it gives the *really* existing deer an *intentional* existence within itself, thereby *intentionally becoming* the thing known. The essence of the being out there in the world is recreated as a being of the mind. And this we call, in common parlance, "having an idea of something." That, in short, is how we know *what* something is. We know *that* something is, however, by judging it *to be*.

What is this judgement of something *to be*? It cannot be solely on account of the five senses, for the senses cannot know or 'judge' anything. That would be like saying, "the eyes see." No, they do not see. Your eyes receive reflected light. *You* see. Nor can one judge a thing *to be* merely by having an idea of the thing, for, as noted, it is perfectly possible to have ideas of things that do not exist. What is it, then, that judges a thing to be? The answer is *you*. You judge things to be. The 'judgement of existence,' as it is sometimes called, is an act of the whole person. Why, indeed, should I suppose that when I act, it is in fact only a part of me that acts, rather than the whole of me? We are not machines, we are organisms, and we act — including the act of knowing a thing — as single, unified agents.

Then ... the seventeenth-century philosopher René Descartes decided to ask a question that never should have been asked: *How do I know that things exist outside my mind?* This is the question of a madman, but unfortunately it was taken seriously by everyone. The seriousness with which his question was considered, rather than making a sane man out of Descartes, turned everyone else mad.

Descartes' solution, famously, was to attempt to retrieve the notion of 'external reality' by attending to the ideas in his mind. The trouble is that, as noted, ideas in the mind are of essences that need not be conjoined with a principle of existence, and they may indeed not correspond to anything out there in the world. Again, one does not know something *to be* by having an idea of its existence, but by judging it *to be*. Real existence, of which we can have no intelligible idea — but rather only judge something *to be* or *not to be* — cannot, then, be conjured up out of the ideas of the mind.

Today, we are so far downstream from Descartes that we think it is reasonable, upon conceiving an idea, to believe that its existential realisation will naturally follow from having such an idea. This

assumption, indeed, is largely behind every mur-
derous utopian regime of the last five centuries to
the now popular belief that one can declare oneself
a member of the other sex and — as if by some
spell — that makes it true.

Due to the way reality is composed, this epistemic error was always a possibility for the one who
thinks about reality. It was finally committed, and
the ensuing carnage has largely wrecked the world.
This error is now an ever-present temptation for the
intellectual. The intellectual is constantly tempted
to turn first to the content of his mind rather than
the world out there. For this reason, the intellectual,
rather than being a guiding light for civilisation,
has become a constant mischief-maker.

There have, however, always been those who have
operated on the assumption that things (*real beings*)
are more real than ideas (*intentional beings*), and those
people are called 'conservatives.' By this, I don't refer
to any particular political movement or economic
position, but merely to those people present in all
societies who have always, without much reflection,
privileged the historical, the real, and the concrete
over the abstract, the theoretical, and the utopian.
Indeed, this, I believe, above any other trait, is what
defines the traditionalist in the broadest sense, and
the reverse of this assumption is what defines all
those proponents of revolutionary mayhem who
comprise the traditionalist's tormentors.

It does not surprise me that the error of so-called
'turning to the subject' — or, as I prefer to put it,
Descartes' mad musing — was committed by a math-
ematician with poor health and a fragile constitu-
tion. I sometimes wonder: would Descartes have
made such a terrible epistemic mistake had he spent
fewer hours working out equations and more time
in trees spying on fallow deer? You see, I think

that anyone who is inclined to the intellectual life is under an obligation to get outdoors. The intellectual who is not an outdoorsman is too great a threat to his fellow man, whom he will no doubt eventually come to plague with his ideas.

Spending those insomniac hours wandering in the woods in the glow of the moon, bidding it farewell as the sun slowly rose to take its place, I found myself in the company of that great deer herd. I crouched down, keeping my dog close to me so that he didn't startle them, and shifted behind a fallen tree where I remained for a long time to watch them bathe in the morning sunbeams that flooded the woods with orange light. It is not good for a writer to be sleep-deprived, but in such circumstances I do well to head outdoors, for the alternative is to sit at home and cogitate, eventually to become another intellectual rascal.

# 3

# THE WILD HUNT

THE WILD HUNT IS A RECURRING European folkloric motif. In Germany and in much of Scandinavia, Odin, the lord of the Norse gods, led the Wild Hunt. In France, it was the ghost of King Herod. In England, the Wild Hunt was led by a great antlered spectre named Herne the Hunter who terrorised farmers and frightened cattle. In Wales, the Wild Huntsman was Arawn, god of the underworld. Whilst chiefly Northern European and often associated with Odin's crazed antics, the Wild Hunt also crops up in Spanish folklore, where a Catalonian nobleman — damned because of his raping of unsuspecting virgins — is said to ride out with his hounds from the gates of hell to momentarily escape the eternal fires. In Italy, the Wild Hunt is led by King Theodoric, an Arian heretic who killed the philosopher and Christian saint, Boethius. In Slovenia, the Hunt follows the springtime sprite, Jarylo, who was brutally murdered by his wife for his adultery (she then built a house out of his mangled body parts); Jarylo forever hunts because of his general proclivity for venery, in more senses than one.

In all these accounts, the Wild Hunt is something diabolical. The pack is often made up of black hounds and wolves, with a great flock of corvids flying over them, making an appalling noise. The hounds drip blood, whining and yelping constantly. The horses are jet black. Valkyries, goblins, trolls, elves, ghouls, and naked harlots all ride along in the demonic hunting party. In nearly all accounts, the Wild Huntsman is frequently replaced with the devil himself. The Hunt, when it arrives, is a terror, and often taken to be an omen, heralding that some happening has empowered the prince of this world.

In 1127, Dom Henry d'Angely was elected as Abbot of the Benedictine monastery of Peterborough. He turned out to be an especially terrible abbot. The contemporaneous *Peterborough Chronicle* tells us that on the night of his abbatial election, the Wild Hunt came to Peterborough (where today, incidentally, the Festival of Hunting takes place every summer):

> Many men both saw and heard a great number of huntsmen hunting. The huntsmen were black, huge, and hideous, and rode on black horses and on black he-goats, and their hounds were jet black, with eyes like saucers, and horrible. This was seen in the very deer park of the town of Peterborough, and in all the woods that stretch from that same town to Stamford, and in the night the monks heard them sounding and winding their horns.

Witnesses said that night after night for many weeks this hellish horde returned to torment the town, a calamity that persisted until Easter Sunday of that year.

The Wild Hunt rages deep in the European psyche. Clearly pagan in origin, we Europeans have failed to shake it off. The Wild Hunt has haunted us, inspiring nightmares in every era. It has pursued us down the centuries. Like so much of our pagan past, however, we were never supposed to cast off the Wild Hunt — but redeem it. Indeed, what is a European if not a baptised pagan? As the Gospel spread, the Wild Hunt became increasingly associated with St Guthlac the Hermit in England, with King Arthur throughout much of France, and with Charlemagne in Germany. The Hunt ceased to be simply a terror and became a moment of redemption and sanctification.

In the first century, the Roman general St Eustace,
whilst out hunting with his hounds, encountered
a great stag between whose antlers was a miraculous crucifix (an exquisite fifteenth-century fresco
depicting this event can be found in Canterbury
Cathedral). Six centuries later, St Hubert under-
went a dramatic conversion due to a similar vision,
and later became the patron saint of hunting. The
monks of St Hubert, in the Northern Lowlands,
specialised in breeding scent hounds which, pre-
dictably, were called St Hubert hounds. To these
hounds the modern-day bloodhound can be traced,
which was itself an important breed for developing
the foxhound, harrier, beagle, and hunting basset.
Traditionally, on St Hubert's Day, a liturgy with
hunting horns would be celebrated, followed by the
blessing of the packs. The hunting Season would
often begin with such liturgical events, too.

When the Season draws to a close, I often find
myself reflecting on the meaning of hunting. Some
hunts have transported me into a timeless experience into which, no doubt, many hunting people
have been taken. It is as if the Wild Hunt, now
a hallowed procession, arrives and gathers one up
into the mystic hunting party, no longer comprised
of ghouls but of all our ancestors who worked to
make the land into a place of peace and dwelling,
cultivating it from a threatening wilderness into
a source of sustenance and a home.

I have regularly been called upon to 'whip-in,' that
is, help to control the pack as they seek to pick up a
trail. On one occasion, our hunt headed into an open
valley flanked by a strip of woodland on either side.
The Huntsman 'cast' the hounds. I went up near the
woods and peered into the dark arboreal halls where
coppiced hazel grew like giant spiders' legs. Two 'couple' (four hounds) became separated, and so, with whip

in hand, I guided them back to the pack, which they quickly located due to the sound of the Huntsman's horn. Into the woods the pack ran, silently sniffing as they worked. Then, on the hillside, in the heart of the woods, they picked up the trail—the sound of their cry echoing through the trees was almost numinous. I found myself in a world as yet unsubordinated to the great machine of modernity, and still bearing the imprint of the centuries upon its face.

Has hunting, though, really been redeemed, or is it as evil as Odin's Wild Hunt would make you believe? Certainly, hunt-saboteurs consider hunting the very epitome of wickedness. Indeed, so much so that they feel wholly justified in putting death-threats through the front doors of hunt followers' homes and threatening to burn down pubs that welcome the hunt—both of which have happened in connection with my own hunt.

Yet few, if any, argue that wildlife management in the countryside must stop altogether. Indeed, when the UK Hunting Act was passed in 2004 (after which hunting with hounds has continued only in pursuit of an artificial trail), no one to my knowledge suggested that the Act should be taken as the first step to ending wildlife management altogether, only that such wildlife was not to be managed by the use of hounds.

A fox, however, can run faster than a foxhound. A hare can run faster than a harrier, beagle, or basset. When quarry is caught, therefore, it is inevitably old or sick, and thus also a threat to the healthy population of its own kind. Moreover, the hunting Season ends as mating begins. Hunting with hounds, then, was a way of managing the population of a given species that was simultaneously discriminatory.[1]

---

[1] Many of the compelling animal welfare arguments in favour of hunting with hounds can be found throughout Pye-Smith's *Rural Wrongs*.

What we are left with now in the United Kingdom
(apart from Northern Ireland, for the time being)
are ways of managing these species that have no
close season and are indiscriminate—using snares or
firearms—making little to no distinction between a
young, healthy, or even pregnant animal and a sick
or old one. Furthermore, such methods often entail
the slow death of the animal over many hours, or
even days, rather than the remarkably quick death
achieved by a pack of hounds. These methods of
managing wildlife are now ubiquitous, and will
naturally continue to increase, since hunting quarry
with hounds has been stopped. There are swathes of
the UK which once had well-managed, healthy fox
populations, where the fox has now almost disappeared altogether.

So, what has the anti-hunting lobby achieved? Well,
they certainly have not improved the situation of the
animals for which they claim to have so much affection, but they have successfully weakened the rural
community, which was so intertwined with the hunt.
All this, it seems, due to childish sentimentalism.

This situation was foreseen by the Victorian
writer D.W. Nash, who gave a voice to the fox in
his poem "The Fox's Prophecy":

> Yet think not, huntsman, I rejoice
> To see the end so near;
> Nor think the sound of horn and hound
> To me a sound of fear...

> Too well I know, by wisdom taught
> The existence of my race
> O'er all wide England's green domain
> Is bound up with the Chase.

> Better in early youth and strength
> The race for life to run,
> Than poisoned like the noxious rat,
> Or slain by felon gun.

Consider also the case of the American mink. This animal was, wrongly, brought to the UK in the 1930s for its fur. Many escaped, and, by the 1960s, there were minks living in most of the nation's rivers. Minks are an invasive species, doing significant damage to the freshwater fish population, and the populations of our beloved waterfowl and songbirds. In response, rural people acted creatively, establishing minkhound packs mostly made up of retired foxhounds. They were effective, killing around 1,500 minks a year. After the Hunting Act, there remains no effective way to manage mink numbers, at least not without doing great harm to other species. Today, there are estimated to be around 110,000 American minks in the UK, causing untold damage.

It was for these reasons among others that Jim Barrington, former Executive Director of the League Against Cruel Sports, who has been involved in animal welfare campaigns for over four decades, 'switched sides' and is now the welfare consultant to the Countryside Alliance and the Council of Hunting Associations. Barrington dispassionately considered the evidence and concluded that the position he had hitherto taken was mistaken.

One answer to what I have written is that we ought to just leave nature to do its own thing, and *we* should get on and do our thing. This, however, assumes that we are not a part of nature, with our own role in relation to other species and the environment in which we have settled. Furthermore, the agricultural and pastoral land that we share with wild animals is not natural in the sense of a wilderness or jungle. It is precisely a creation of the human ingenuity that, over many centuries, has transformed and cultivated the wild into an orderly and reliable source of food and apparel. We must, in truth, manage what we have made.

If what I say is true, and the 'animal cruelty' argument does not stand up to scrutiny, as I claim, then why are we prohibited by the law from hunting quarry with hounds throughout most of the UK? As noted, those who campaigned for the Hunting Act did not campaign for an end to wildlife management altogether. So, what is it about *hunting with hounds* that was deemed so objectionable? This takes us back to my passing reflection on the intoxicating experience of being carried up into the Wild Hunt. For the anti-hunting lobby, what is *really* objectionable is that, over the centuries, rural communities have found a way of managing wildlife which is also thoroughly enjoyable. They think that if animals must be killed, then those doing the killing should at least feel miserable about it.

There is something to this argument with which I have great sympathy. Given that 'animal rights' do not exist, any sound ethical argument against hunting must focus on the person hunting rather than the animal. 'Animal rights' cannot exist, for animals do not enjoy the innate faculties to make moral claims over things or claim moral powers to fulfil duties by which they deem themselves bound. A tigress that abandons its cubs is not a miscreant and does not deserve punishment. Animals are not moral agents, and therefore cannot have rights. Does this mean, then, that we are free to torture animals for our amusement? No, it does not. Not because the animal can make a moral claim on us, but because torturing an animal will morally corrupt us as the agents of such an act. In fact, the desire to torture animals is an early sign of psychopathy.

The anti-hunting lobby purports to be concerned with animal welfare, but in truth their object of attention is the psychology of the people hunting, and in this they are absolutely correct. This is the crucial issue: Does hunting with hounds make us crueller? Wildlife management, which entails the killing of animals, may indeed make us crueller. In turn, the great challenge is both to find a method of killing animals that kills them quickly (and is therefore not unnecessarily cruel), and also raises the activity of wildlife management into the realm of culture and ritual, in which the animal's death is no longer the focus, but rather enjoyment of community, ceremony, and the land. Both imperatives are satisfied by hunting with hounds. So much is this the case that 'a good day's hunting' may just as likely be one during which no quarry is caught (indeed, hunting with hounds has only increased in popularity since the Hunting Act, after which, as noted, hunting has continued in pursuit of an artificial trail).

I stress the point of wildlife management because it conveys that hunting with hounds has real practical value. In an age when communal membership, tradition, ritual, locality, even nature itself, remain obscure for many people, such arguments are important. But in the hunting field, if one were to ask the followers or staff why they come out to hunt, they would not say 'wildlife management' or 'the kill.' They would say that they have a tenderness for the hunting community, for watching the hounds work, for the farmers who welcome the hunt onto their land, and for the rural way of life. The emotional life of people who hunt, then, is not something over which we need to worry; the psychological stability of those who terrorise fieldsporting pensioners, however, is far more questionable.

If the real joy of the person who hunts is derived, in short, from the experience of the countryside, can the desire of the hunter be satisfied by the activity of the hiker? Hiking, or leisure-walking,

emerged in the late-eighteenth century precisely
in response to the rationalism and industrialism
that had warped our relationship with nature to
the point that we no longer saw ourselves as a part
of it. People, intuiting that modernity had severed
them from the world, went wandering about in it
like visitors from another planet. This can still be
seen in the respective garb of these two types of
people whom one might encounter in the countryside: the hunting coat, tweed or 'ratcatcher' of the
hunter and the florescent synthetic materials of the
hiker testify to two different ways of relating to
the rural environment. One is that of a dwelling
person who is a part of the land, the other is that
of a foreign visitor who has dropped in for a rare
taste of reality. I thoroughly enjoy a long hike or a
gentle ramble through the countryside, but the point
remains that those who *only* know the countryside
from this perspective struggle to see the landscape
from *inside*, so to speak.

Over my years of hunting, there have been
moments when I've been up on a hillside or deep
in the belly of a valley, and I have suddenly heard
the hounds 'speak.' At that moment, the countryside
thunders with their cry, and I unexpectedly become
aware of myself. This self-awareness strikes me as
unusual because when hunting one almost ceases
to be aware of oneself altogether. One's consciousness gets absorbed into the collective thrill of the
Wild Hunt. And in the midst of it, one becomes a
part of the land. At such moments, after hours of
being awake and present to the world, I slip back
into the slumber of self-awareness — self-obsession,
even — that characterises modern man's condition.
In response, I grip my hunting whip and refocus on
the hounds, waking myself up again to the world
and returning to reality.

# 4

# THE MAGICAL KINGDOM
# OF MUSHROOMS

B IG, TALL PARASOL MUSHROOMS—
my favourite wild mushroom—dotted about
in huge rings across the meadow. Returning to my car, I collected my foraging knife (a
curved knife with a horse-hair brush attached to
the handle) and canvas sack and began to harvest
the magnificent fungal crop. My wife crouched
beside me, and our children darted about finding
more hidden fairy-rings onto which we could move
next. The late summer sun was setting, and soon
I had our dinner on my back. We didn't strip the
field, but we had more than enough mushrooms.

Once home, I checked the mushrooms for mag-
gots, then chopped them, fried them in butter, and
added garlic, pepper, salt, sherry, double cream,
and a few shavings of Gruyère cheese. Soon, we
had a large bowl of something loosely resembling
a mushroom stroganoff, and the four families we'd
invited over were scooping the dish out and piling
it upon cake-like sourdough that I'd grabbed from
the farm shop down the road. Our meal went down
very well with large glasses of Romanian Pinot noir.
Behold: life as it ought to be. Families gathered
around a table eating locally foraged mushrooms
on locally baked bread, chatting and making merry
late into the night.

While the hysterical lockdown politics of 2020-21
made such humble aspirations of free-association
and friendship difficult, it was in fact an accidental

effect of the lockdowns that brought us all together
that evening. Like many others, I took advantage
of our nationwide house-imprisonment and learned
to forage for mushrooms without poisoning myself
and my loved ones. In fact, spending so much
time out in the fields and woods, I was amazed
to discover that we reside within a wellspring of
wild, delicious food. The landscape became for me,
besides the realm of beauty it had always been, a
source of immediate sustenance, and this changed
my relationship with it as I became more—so to
speak—one with it.

Our natural union with our surroundings, which
all other mammals uncritically feel, and which we
have distorted by our technological departure from
the world of which we were supposed to make a
home, is a union that we can begin to reclaim by
becoming students of mushrooms. I mean this quite
straightforwardly: mushrooms are teachers, and we
ought to learn from them.

Fungi comprise a kingdom. This is a fact that
most of us do not acknowledge. We are used to
talking of the animal kingdom and the plant kingdom, but not of the fungi kingdom. Fungi are not
plants; they are more like animals than plants.
Unlike plants, they cannot make their own food,
and they are largely predatory. Strictly speaking,
mushrooms are not foraged but 'hunted.' We likely
do not think of fungi as a kingdom because fungi
are hidden away—vast mycelial networks under our
feet—and we only consider them when we see their
upward-hanging fruits, that is, their mushrooms.

Hunting mushrooms is very dangerous. Whereas
the hunting of most quarry entails danger only
for the one hunted, many mushrooms will take
their predators down with them. The way that
these mushrooms take their victims' lives is also

inexpressibly awful. Take for example the death cap, or the destroying angel, both of which do not look dissimilar to one of Europe's yummiest mushrooms, the St George's mushroom. Both deadly toadstools will make you vomit for twenty-four hours. Then, just when you think you're past it all and on the mend, they poison your blood and shut down each of your vital organs until you perish in excruciating pain.

For this reason, at first, I learned to identify and hunt only a few mushrooms from books and manuals, ones with no poisonous lookalikes: parasols, giant puffballs, field blewits... Then, to advance further, I went on several courses with expert mycologists with whom I made contact through a local forager (a nice lady who lives on a canal boat and is known in these parts as 'the hedge-witch'). Through this initiation into the mysterious fungal kingdom, I learned to hunt fairy-ring champignons, common puffballs, penny buns, wood ears, shaggy inkcaps, horse and field mushrooms, chanterelles, amethyst deceivers, and shelf mushrooms like beefsteaks and chicken of the woods.

Learning the craft of mushroom hunting also provided a certain cultural formation, this skill being one that was widespread among our pre-industrial forebears. Mushrooms are deeply embedded in the European folk imagination. Indeed, the red and white-spotted fly agaric mushroom is a staple for children's fairytale illustrations. It is widely believed that Father Christmas's famous outfit may be traced back to the fly agaric. For centuries, the Sami reindeer-herders of Lapland have used a special technique to enjoy the mind-altering effects of fly agaric consumption whilst avoiding the consequences of its poisonous properties. Their trick was to feed these mushrooms to their reindeer—which relished the taste of them and were unaffected by their toxicity—which then urinated out a psyche-delic beverage that the Sami would drink. Hal-lucinogenic deer piss might not sound appetising, but there was no better brew to get them through the polar night, and hence it was highly prized. It is believed by many that this custom has some connection to portraying St Nicholas dressed in the colours of the fly agaric, soaring out of Lap-land, pulled through the air by a herd of reindeer. Fly agarics are very striking mushrooms; when I stumbled upon a bright red fly agaric in the woods near my home, my first thought was that a fairy or pixie must be close by.

In his marvellous book, *Entangled Life*, mycol-ogist Merlin Sheldrake reveals how psychedelic mushrooms are leading the way as powerful aids to therapeutic care.[1] Many people have reported that 'mushroom therapy,' using psilocybin 'magic' mushrooms, has enabled them to move past serious trauma or conquer life-stifling fears. There is also increasing evidence that these mushrooms, used in a careful and controlled manner, can help people overcome grave addictions, even addictions to her-oin and crystal meth. There are wonderful passages in Sheldrake's book that describe how the use of psilocybin mushrooms has allowed people to break out of nihilistic or materialistic conceptions of the world and adopt a perspective that they are inclined to describe as 'religious,' 'spiritual,' or 'mystical.'

A friend once described to me his experience of taking psychoactive mushrooms as "a total take-over of the brain's right hemisphere." Readers of the psy-chiatrist and neuroscientist Iain McGilchrist will of

---

[1] See Merlin Sheldrake, *Entangled Life: How Fungi Make Our Worlds, Change Our Minds, and Shape Our Futures* (London: Vin-tage, 2020).

course understand what my friend was getting at.[2] As it happens, I once personally raised this with Iain when I visited him at his home on the Isle of Skye. He explained that what was more likely happening during mushroom-induced psychedelic experiences was the suspension of much activity in the brain's frontal lobes altogether, which would help explain the "oneness" with the environment that people often express in the reports of their 'trips' — a 'oneness,' or lack of conscious individuality, perhaps comparable to that which is normally felt by a wild animal with no developed frontal lobes.

Be that as it may, besides mental health, mushrooms are increasingly being used for health in general. For example, due to the pioneering work of mycologist and medical researcher Paul Stamets, many are using ground turkey tail mushroom in capsules to maintain proper immune system function during cancer treatment — a use of this mushroom that may have saved the life of Stamets's own mother when she had breast cancer. Only now are we in the West beginning to discover the healing properties of chaga, cordyceps, maitake, oyster, shiitake, and other mushrooms. For years now, I have personally been using various mushrooms for my own health, and back in 2021 I shook off post-Covid 'brain fog' by consuming dried reishi and lion's mane mushrooms.

Sheldrake's book presents how fungi are connected with everything else, even our own bodies which rely on complex fungal systems for even their most basic wellbeing. Long before mammals walked the earth, the free-moving algae-like plant species that left the oceans and became the trees

---

[2] See Iain McGilchrist, *The Master and His Emissary: The Divided Brain and the Making of the Western World* (London: Yale University Press, 2019).

and greenery we see around us today, did so because
they partnered with mycelial structures across the
open lands. Trees and plant life strongly depend
on the mycelium that form an underground world,
one as alien to us as our ocean depths.

Only now, through rigorous experimentation,
are we beginning to grasp the complexity of the
relationship between mycelium and everything else.
As you walk through the woods, these underground
networks send out signals to the trees and plants,
bringing your presence to their 'attention.' Just
as you are aware of the woodland all around, so
the woodland is in some sense aware of you being
within it. Mycelium can also send signals across
their subterranean web, or to other networks of
mycelium altogether. How? We don't really know,
but some speculate that this is done by the releasing
of a salt solution, whilst others believe it is done
by electric waves.

Perhaps it ought not to surprise us that spotted
mushrooms, toadstools, and fairy-rings are a recurring subject of European folklore. There is something about mushrooms that is *enchanting*. Indeed,
the more one studies mushrooms and learns the
signs to track and hunt them, the more enchanting
they become. And surprisingly, when fungi are subjected to scientific scrutiny, they do not lose their
enchanting character but rather the enchantment
is intensified — and what is more, they re-enchant
everything else.

Mushrooms really are teachers. The theist argues
that everything is connected by its shared intelligibility since everything emanates from the mind of
God and is granted existence by Him, an existence
that indirectly participates in His own *necessary* existence. Everything is also connected, one may argue,
on account of the consciousness that *we* bring to the

world, a consciousness that allows us to look upon the world from without, and represent it within ourselves for our reflection, that it may become, as it were, a secondary world within us. Fungi teach us, however, that purposive and meaningful ways of seeing the world as fundamentally interconnected due to *mind* (both divine and created), are actually reflected 'extramentally' in the world itself. Fungi aren't just a kingdom in their own right; they are the kingdom that bridges kingdoms. Everything, from the vast forests and jungles to the most basic operations of your own body, is bound up with the life of fungi.

One of the maladies of modernity is that of privileging abstract categories over concrete realities. You can only begin to understand fungi, as Sheldrake brilliantly conveys in his book, once you have privileged reality and grasped that reality is a structure of inter-reliant realities, not isolated abstractions. Reality is comprised of things that are both things in themselves and participant-things that share in a mysterious complexus of symbiotic and interdependent entities, the boundaries between which are blurred to say the least. That this is the true nature of reality, which we only discover once we have returned from our abstractions back to reality, is taught to us no better than by fungi.

In 1970, British archaeologist John M. Allegro published *The Sacred Mushroom and the Cross,* in which he argued that Jesus Christ never existed but was in fact a deliberately contrived mythological creation of early Christians who were under the influence of psychoactive mushrooms. [3] Whilst I agree with

---

[3] See John M. Allegro, *The Sacred Mushroom and The Cross: A study of the nature and origins of Christianity within the fertility cults of the ancient Near East* (Scottsdale, Arizona: Gnostic Media Research & Publishing; 40th Anniversary Edition, 2009).

Philip Jenkins, professor of history at Baylor University, that Allegro's book is "possibly the single most ludicrous book on Jesus scholarship by a qualified academic," and downright offensive to pious ears as well, it does not surprise me that fungi have made their way into religious controversy just as they've made their way into everything else. There does seem to be something 'otherworldly' about mushrooms, and they recurrently adopt a place on the border of religious experience.

Mushrooms, one might suggest, are illustrative of the providential goodness of God. A chief reason why northern Europeans suffer so many colds and coughs during autumn and winter is because they are vitamin and nutrient deficient and their immune systems are struggling. But, as the sun vanishes behind thick, dark clouds, and the cold comes to rattle our bones, up from beneath our world's surface come the fruits of that mysterious underground world. Mushrooms are packed with vitamins B, C, and D, anti-inflammatories, and antioxidants, as well as selenium for protection against cell damage and infections, and magnesium for proper nerve function and energy production. At the very moment when the sky above our heads can no longer give us what we need, the earth beneath comes alive, delivering—like manna in the desert—what we require to keep us going. Moreover, the earth provides us with something that can be dried and kept for months on end without losing its nutritional value. The 'fittingness' of this is not only indicative of the existence of God but of theodicy—that is, His *goodness*.

Many have been predicting that our mass, globalised, hyper-industrialised food production trade is on the verge of collapse. Perhaps they're right. This might mean, of course, that we shall eat less processed food, more garden vegetables, and perhaps pork from the fattened pig that was in the backyard rather than from some distant, cramped creature in a metal container that's been kept alive on a stream of antibiotics. Moreover, as the healthcare industry continues to undermine itself, that too may collapse. Whatever struggles await us, mushrooms may have an important role in securing our flourishing. These 'superfoods' are easily found growing wild (if you know what you are doing) and effortlessly cultivated domestically. Mushrooms are free, delicious, and their medicinal properties are yet to be fully revealed. In navigating through future troubles, let us not ignore this hidden kingdom.

# 5

# WESTERN CIVILISATION AND DOGS

A YOUNG COUPLE, PROBABLY IN their early thirties, walk the ancient Ridgeway path together in rural Buckinghamshire. He holds her hand protectively; she is wrapped in the straps of a baby sling, her free hand raised to caress the head of her little one. This vision of marital affection and newly emerging parental devotion, set on the backdrop of some of England's most beautiful countryside, would warm the heart of any onlooker.

My wife and I, walking some feet behind, caught up with them as the young mother stopped to attend to the apple of her eye. "My baby," we overheard her saying, "Are you waking up, my darling? Are you hungry?" The attentive husband had already taken off his rucksack and from it was delivering a bottle of milk. As we passed them, we smiled and looked warmly at their baby, only to find ourselves staring at a cockerpoo.

I like dogs. Indeed, when we witnessed this harrowing spectacle, our cherished whippet Pico was trotting alongside us. But so were our children, and we could tell the difference.

Westerners have a fascinating relationship with dogs, a relationship that does not seem to have existed in any other civilisation. The Japanese samurai always had their fighting dogs, Tibetan monks their little apsos; the Arabs have ever coursed gazelle and jackal on the dunes with their salukis; but the integration of dog-keeping into every aspect of culture is something uniquely Western, and especially English.

Perhaps our affection for dogs is an effect of the Christian religion. Dogs seldom appear in Holy Scripture, but when they do, they are signs of fidelity, victory, or healing. In the Bible's two Books of Kings, when the Baal-worshiping Jezebel—believing her husband's political power should be arbitrary and unaccountable—had Naboth the viticulturalist murdered in order to snatch his property, the dogs of the city would not eat his corpse but licked it in atonement instead. The same dogs, however, later delighted in gobbling up Jezebel's body. A dog accompanied Tobias and the archangel Raphael in their quest to find Tobias a wife, a successful expedition that led to a happy marriage after a dead fish was used to deliver the lady in question from demonic infestation (it's a great story—Protestants are really missing out, since they don't recognise the Book of Tobit as canonical). In the New Testament, dogs attend to the sores of the good man Lazarus, whom Christ later describes as enjoying the beatific vision.

Maybe it is due to their scattered place in Holy Writ that dogs became a motif of European sacred culture. St Roch, the pilgrim saint, is always depicted with a dog at his feet, ready to give first aid in the style of Lazarus's canine friends. The great St Philip Howard, when sent to the Tower for his loyalty to the ancient Faith, was permitted to take his hunting dog with him, who has been present in depictions of his master ever since. The association of holiness and dogs reached its extremity in the fourteenth century when religious devotion to a greyhound, St Guinefort, developed in eastern France. There were attempts by the Inquisition to suppress the cult of St Guinefort, but veneration of this hound persisted until the 1930s.

Perhaps there is only an accidental connection between Christianity and the role of dogs in our culture, but the fact remains that dogs have a special place in Western civilisation, unseen elsewhere. In medieval secular art, dogs were exclusively depicted doing a job, usually hunting; but by the Renaissance it was popular, when having one's portrait painted, to have one's dog standing in the picture. Veronese's *Boy with a Greyhound* is an obvious example, or Bartolomeo Passerotti's *Portrait of a Man with a Dog*. This theme continued into the following century, exemplified by Van Dyck's family portraits for King Charles I in which toy spaniels, miniature greyhounds, and enormous mastiffs are all featured, carefully placed to convey something about the people with whom they sit. In the eighteenth century, the wealthy English parliamentarians for whom Pompeo Batoni painted portraits wanted their sighthounds by their feet, just like the ruling royalist nobles of the previous century, indicating that these Whigs were now the true bearers of political power.

Something odd also happened during this period. Paintings emerged of dogs *without* any people. These were not just artistic studies, like those of wild animals or still lifes; these were *portraits* for which the dogs' owners paid a lot of money. John Wootton's *A Grey Spotted Hound* and George Stubb's *White Poodle in a Punt* come to mind. Soon we would have Briton Rivière's *Requiescat* in which the human is not the subject — indeed the human is a corpse in the background. In the foreground of this painting sits a magnificent bloodhound, whose devotion, faithfulness — *personality,* even — is the subject. This is an idea taken up and presented again in Landseer's *Old Shepherd's Chief Mourner*, and conveyed differently in his famous depiction of Bob, a newfoundland who was celebrated in Victorian society, being made a member

Veronese, *Boy with a Greyhound*, 1570s

Bartolomeo Passerotti, *Portrait of a Man with a Dog*, ca. 1586

Anthony van Dyck, *Five Eldest Children of Charles I*, 1637

Pompeo Batoni, *Portrait of John Talbot, Later First Earl Talbot*, 1773

John Wootton, *A Grey Spotted Hound*, 1738

George Stubbs, *White Poodle in a Punt*, c. 1780

Briton Rivière, *Requiescat*, 1888

Edwin Landseer, *Old Shepherd's Chief Mourner*, 1837

of a charitable trust and awarded various medals.

We see here a gradual transformation of the role
of dogs in our society. In the classical Western conception, the dog held a privileged place somewhere
between an instrument and an extension of human
personality. All dogs had jobs, jobs that made the
lives of their masters either possible or easier. It is
by these jobs that dogs are still categorised today.
All breeds are either hounds (hunting dogs), gun-
dogs, terriers (ground dogs), pastoral dogs, working
dogs (guards or labourers), or toy dogs. Even those
little pooches in the last group had important jobs,
keeping their masters and mistresses warm as 'sleeve
dogs' or working as household ratters.

In order for dogs to do their jobs, however, they
had to enter into the personality of their owners. In
this way they are completely different from horses,
cats, or any other creature to which we have given
a place in our world. Observe a shepherd working
with his collie and you will see that his human
agency has been imparted to his dog, a creature that
has become a near-perfect extension of the shepherd,
allowing him to spread himself and his causal power
across whole fields from a stationary position.

Dogs featured in portraits of humans because
of this unique relationship. The dog is there in
the portrait as an aspect of the personality of the
human, telling the spectator something about him
that could not be conveyed were the dog absent.
Look at Van Dyck's portrait of *James Stuart, Duke of
Richmond and Lennox*. Were his greyhound not there,
a whole complexus of the young duke's character
would remain undisclosed to us. We know from the
dog that the duke is not, at least, a cruel master,
that he is a composed man in possession of gentle-
manly qualities, and we know this largely because
of the dog. The dog's presence in the painting does

Anthony van Dyck, *James Stuart,*
*Duke of Richmond and Lennox,* ca. 1634

not tell you much about the dog, but a lot about his master to whom he is wholly directed and whose personality he is there to transmit.

A dog wants to 'understand' its master and unite its desire to its master's will. This finds an analogue in human relationships. Essential to the possession of personhood is the capacity to go beyond the self and make one's own the perspective of another. As Roger Scruton argued in *The Face of God*, we cannot know a person by looking at his elbow or his shin—we encounter the person in the face.[1] Faces form the magnetic field within which persons rest like loadstars. And it is in that I-You encounter (to use the terminology of the great Jewish philosopher Martin Buber) that we cease to be just human beings, mere examples of a species, and become unique, irreplaceable, non-transferable *persons*. We are persons inasmuch as we are persons for each other. Scruton once told me that, in his view, dogs sit somewhere between brutes and persons: dogs do, in part, enter into a kind of relatedness with us to adopt our perspectives.

When a man throws a stick for his dog, the dog will look for *that* stick and is not content to pick up another. In this way, dogs transcend their instrumentality, and they engage with us as quasi-moral creatures that seem to have a share in our interior lives. It is this remarkable capacity for quasi-interpersonal engagement, however, that makes them so morally dangerous. It was their jobs, their subordination to our needs—the fact that we could always see them from the perspective of utility—that protected us from a purely sentimental relationship with them. Now that they have lost their jobs, we have become ensnared.

---

[1] See Roger Scruton, *The Face of God* (London: Continuum, 2012), 80.

Fundamentally, dogs justified their existence in human society by serving us. To serve us, they had to enter into our perspective, according to their capacity, and become extensions of our personalities. By our dogs, we were able to extend ourselves into the non-rational world of the animal. And simultaneously, dogs were ennobled by being elevated to share in our rationality.

By this relationship, dogs helped to keep us from the ever-present temptation to cut ourselves adrift from the natural world of which we are a part, which they still inhabit, and without which we cannot be happy. European culture, for all its music halls, theatres, and art galleries, never ignored the need for therapeutic treatment against this unnatural temptation, and hence nurtured remedies like hunting, hiking, and riding. Indeed, part of the genius of Europe has been — contra Jean-Jacques Rousseau — that of celebrating these earthy activities in its high culture, rather than exploiting high culture to set up a supposed dichotomy between them (as Rousseau did). In our outdoor pursuits we have ever been accompanied by our canine companions.

Having lost their jobs, however, dogs have continued to inhabit our world without any purpose beyond enjoying the quasi-interpersonal relatedness that developed between us and them so that they could do their jobs properly. Now, we can warm ourselves by directing our emotion at our dogs, for they, like mirrors, beam our emotion back at us. In an age of sentimentalism, the jobless dog is a colossal moral danger.

Sentimentalism is false emotion. It is that emotional feeling that purports to be outward facing, but is actually self-directed and kindled for the purpose of enjoying cheap consolation. Sentimentalism is the autoeroticism of the emotional life.

The neo-revolutionaries that torment the modern world provide good examples of sentimentalism. The question of whether the activists are fulfilling their declared goals is not what is ultimately important; what matters is the intense feeling they have of standing on the 'right side of history.' Their chaotic exhibitions of passion are self-didactic, teaching them that they are who they think they should be.

Thus, sentimentalism buys up counterfeit goodness, bypassing the imperative to acquire virtue, attend to conscience, be called to account, master oneself, confess one's failings, atone for one's evils, and make terrible sacrifices. The behaviour of the perpetual adolescents of late modernity is the product of a Disneyland education combined with rage. The personal struggle to overcome sentimentalism is long and difficult. There is, however, a shortcut: kids.

The arrival of children is transformative. Unless one is completely morally bankrupt, children have the effect of making one grow up quickly, accept responsibility, develop some self-control, attend to concrete necessities, and put oneself second. No decent father is the father he thinks he should be. Every good father is deeply aware of his parental shortcomings. That is what is so wonderful about fatherhood. A good father knows that he must grow because, in a thousand indirect ways, his children call him to account, inviting him to stand in judgement over himself, accuse himself, and resolve to be a better Dad tomorrow. This sphere of accountability is the interior territory where dogs cannot go. A dog will always gaze at you with big eyes, hanging tongue, and communicate that you are great, regardless of how much of an ass you actually are.

Dogs, when looking up at their masters, come as close as any sub-rational brute can to executing an act of worship. For the modern sentimental soul, the presence of a dog is like a drug. A dog can become a perfect surrogate for every possible relationship, injecting with each tail-wag that fix of emotional consolation without demanding any of the personal growth required by a real bond.

Now, at peak decadence and degeneracy, our culture has accepted as normal the emergence of human-canine 'families.' It is not uncommon for people with dogs to describe them as their 'children,' or for couples with one or more dogs to describe themselves as a 'family.' This is profoundly disordered.

Occasionally, my whippet takes off after some quarry halfway down a field, and in that moment I am reminded of his job, the job for which — over a few thousand years — humans bred wolves into creatures that can run down other animals at forty miles per hour. I am reminded in that moment that, as much as I love my dog, he is doing something deeply unhuman, of which I have no experience, out of which he will not grow. He will never reflect on his impulses, nor criticise me for failing to protect him from them. When I see my dog do that for which he was bred, I remember that, in fact, the relationship that exists between us is almost wholly in my head. Between my whippet and me there will always be an immense and uncrossable abyss, for the singular reason that my pet is not a person. The shepherd knows this about his collie, and the foxhunter about his foxhounds. To paraphrase Wittgenstein, if my whippet could talk, I would not be able to understand him.

Perhaps, in this age of sentimentalism, the worst thing that could have happened in dogdom is the founding of the cockerpoo. Cockerpoos have no job. They are bred solely to be living teddy bears, showering their owners with constant energetic affection and, with their non-shedding coats, leaving no dog hair to disturb the pristine showroom house, that ubiquitous Huxleyan, synthetic dwelling which modern people prefer, severed from the natural world which mature people invite inside.

The special role of dogs in Western civilisation is one of its many achievements. But as our civilisation unravels, so too its delights become severed from their roots and go rotten. Now, the great work of conservatives like me is not so much to conserve, for so much has been lost that there is little to conserve at all. The *great work* is that of recovering, restoring, and redeeming what has been lost. The place of the dog in our Western civilisation stands in desperate need of redemption. One solution would be that of resituating hunting at the heart of our common culture again. By this, most dogs would get their jobs back, and a fine therapy for overcoming sentimentalism towards animals can be found in the cultural celebration of killing them.

In truth, I have no exhaustive solution to the problem I have raised beyond stressing the wider moral transformation that our culture so urgently needs. Dog ownership is among the many joys of my life, and it grieves me that such an innocent pleasure has aided our downfall.

# 6

# TROPHY HUNTING AND THE ABOLITION OF POLITICS

KILLING AND EATING SOME OF Britain's big mammals is a profound source of joy in my life. It is not just the sport; I also appreciate how deer stalking locks one into a rural community of other field sportsmen, as well as landowners, tenant farmers, and family butchers. But increasingly, I have also been looking to other countries' wild animals and wondering what I might bag were I to travel abroad to hunt with a rifle. Perhaps I have, without being aware that this was happening to me, become an aspiring trophy hunter.

The term, of course, is somewhat misleading, not to mention controversial. What so-called 'trophy hunters' do—or ought to do—is travel to different locations so that they might discover for themselves the wild parts of those lands, be immersed in the hunting traditions of those countries, and execute their very demanding and long-cultivated skill. The 'trophy' itself—the hunted animal's head, brought home to be displayed on a wall—in the minds of most such hunters is a mere piece of memorabilia, collected so as not to forget the event, and as a way of continually honouring the beast whose life was taken.

What is widely termed trophy hunting is one of those very rare things in this fallen and troubled world: a near-unqualified good. As a rule, I do not like the term 'trophy hunting' because it misleads people, but I'll use it here because it is used by others.

The first notion that people need to understand is
that animals, in the wild, die very horrible deaths.
For example, a deer that is not killed by being
wounded by a competing member of its species,
caught by a predator, or eaten from the inside-out
by parasites, simply starves to death. This is how
most British deer die. Indeed, that is how most her-
bivore species throughout the world die, including
elephants. Over the course of their lives, they grind
down their teeth until they cannot digest food any
longer; then, they grow weaker and weaker, weighed
down by huge stomachs bloated with undigested
plants, until wounds finally open up and disease
takes over their bodies. In short, they slowly rot
to death. In the case of large African herbivores,
they eventually collapse with weakness, at which
point most are torn to pieces by jackals, hyenas,
or lions, or eaten alive by carrion birds. Thus, no
greater fortune can an ageing wild animal obtain
than a bullet to the neck or the heart. And such
hunting is not only good for the individual that
dies, but for the other members of its species, who
are rescued from the threat of disease that such an
animal brings to its kind.

Some trophy hunters are extremely wealthy, and
they introduce eye-watering amounts of money
into the areas where they hunt. There are innumerable stories of wildlife parks in Africa rapidly
extending their boundaries by purchasing land
with money from trophy hunting. Many species
have been brought back from near-extinction due
to this sport. In some parts of Africa, habitat that
can sustain elephants — animals which consume
astonishing amounts of vegetation and are extremely
destructive — has been significantly increased by
inviting wealthy big game hunters to shoot old
bull elephants, whose heads look magnificent in a

large hallway. These old creatures were thus saved from the appalling 'natural' death described above and were simultaneously the means to extremely important conservation efforts.

Half a century ago, the white rhino was nearly extinct. In 1960, these creatures in South Africa were numbered at only 840, and it was illegal to hunt them. By 1968, the country had only managed to get the population up to around a thousand, at which point hunting rhinos was reopened. Due to the growing market for rhino hunting, landowners intentionally sought to populate their lands with these animals. Their number has now increased to almost 20,000. The financial incentives derived from trophy hunting have made South Africa home to 93 percent of the world's white rhinos. This is just one of many, many examples that reveal trophy hunting to be a fundamental driver of animal welfare and conservation. Conversely, Kenya, which banned hunting in 1977, has since seen a 70 percent reduction in its wildlife.

Once a successful hunting industry is established in an area of Africa, it becomes necessary to stop all poaching, which if allowed to continue, destroys the main source of income. Unscrupulous forms of hunting are hence prevented to protect the kind of legal, ethical hunting that not only supports the economy of the place but underpins positive conservation efforts. Many rural communities had largely seen wildlife as an obstacle either to expanding farmland or urbanisation, and therefore they sought to cull as many large mammals as possible. Now, such communities partly rely on the hunting industry for a growing economy. Consequently, in many such areas, it is the local communities that are spearheading efforts to protect animals which they once saw as rivals.

Beyond the financial and conservationist aspects, trophy hunting also undergirds a vital food source. For example, in Zambia alone, where over 60 percent of the population lives in extreme poverty, trophy hunting has considerably increased food security by annually providing more than 286,000 pounds of meat to rural communities adjacent to hunting areas. Undermining this food source by curtailing trophy hunting, either directly or indirectly, would entail serious food shortages for these people.

In sum, trophy hunting is good for the hunted animal. It is good for the unhunted animals. It is good for habitat protection and conservation. It is good for the local communities. It is good for the tourist industry of the country in which it takes place. It is good for the prevention of poaching. And it is good for the trophy hunting sportsman, who can spend his money doing what he loves, money that goes into the local economy of the—more likely than not—developing country.

In 2022, in a letter to *The Guardian*, a number of prominent British academics highlighted the considerable "conservation dividends supported by sustainable hunting," and they noted that attacks on such activities would "risk decreasing animal welfare and imperilling biodiversity."[1] The letter went on:

> Evidence shows that removing regulated trophy hunting—and the incentives it creates for conservation—without having viable funded alternatives ready can lead to greater losses of wildlife, due to subsequent increases in illegal, unsustainable and inhumane killings of animals using snares, dogs,

---

[1] Adam Hart et al., "Regulated trophy hunting aids wildlife conservation," *The Guardian*, April 7, 2022, https://www.theguardian.com/world/2022/apr/07/regulated-trophy-hunting-aids-wildlife-conservation.

local weapons and poisons. A single trophy-hunted lion generates worldwide media attention, but the daily snaring and poisoning of lions in areas where they have little local value is largely ignored. Simplistic solutions to complex problems rarely work.

Academic and conservationist Dr Catherine E. Semcer has suffered criticism for her public defence of trophy hunting.[2] "If we are to reverse the decline of a million or more species toward extinction, then the most fundamental action that must be taken is the conservation of habitat," she has stated. And it's not trophy hunting that is jeopardising the future of animal habitats in Africa. Quite the reverse — it is industry and agriculture, as Semcer explains:

> In much of the world, especially in emerging markets like Africa, habitat conservation depends on making wildlife economically competitive with other land uses. Habitat conversion and degradation — particularly due to crop farming and the herding of livestock — are among the top threats to species conservation in Africa and around the globe. Reducing the incentive to transform wildlands into pastures and farms by clearing woodlands and killing wildlife that prey on livestock or compete for forage is essential to conservation.[3]

In short, to quote the economist Thomas Sowell, "There are no solutions, only ever trade-offs." Trophy hunting in Africa, Semcer notes, has provided

---

[2] See Catherine E. Semcer, "Conservationists should support trophy hunting," PERC.org, September 6, 2019, https://www.perc.org/2019/09/06/conservationists-should-support-trophy-hunting/.
[3] Ibid.

incentives to conserve areas of wildlife habitat more than six times the size of the US National Park System. "This includes nearly 50 million acres of private hunting reserves in South Africa that form a market-based conservation estate comprising 16.8% of the country's total land area."[4]

Semcer lists a great many examples of trophy hunting dramatically improving the lives of African communities, which in turn have mobilised to develop security and conservation efforts to protect those animals that sportsmen come from afar to shoot. I cannot here reproduce Semcer's extensive and comprehensive account of the good that trophy hunting does throughout Africa and beyond, nor her wide-ranging arguments for why trophy hunting has no realistic substitute, nor her many concerns regarding the catastrophe that would befall wildlife conservation across much of the world were trophy hunters to suffer adverse legislation from their own countries, but I strongly encourage readers to do some studying of the topic. Unfortunately, but not unsurprisingly, few people consider trophy hunting with the approach of disinterested analysis, choosing rather to form conclusions from mere emotional impulse.

In 2019, 133 conservation researchers and practitioners signed a letter that was published in *Science Magazine*. This letter highlighted why the trophy hunting bans that have been debated in the US, UK, and the European Parliament are gravely ill-advised. Recently, the UK saw a bill go through its parliament aiming to ban the importation of hunting trophies into the country. This bill was passed with the backing of a so-called Conservative government in March 2023 and at the time of my writing is being scrutinised in the House of Lords.

---

[4] Ibid.

It is bad enough that we are making the capital error that all decaying civilisations have made, namely assuming that everything that may conceivably be disliked on moral grounds — spurious or not — can be fixed with some legislative or bureaucratic solution. What is perhaps worse, however, is that our activist and political classes hold that they can opine about anything they like, irrespective of understanding, and then transcribe their ill-informed opinion into law.

Of course, much of this is mere virtue-signalling. Politicians who loudly condemn trophy hunting, knowing that they have the support of the population's majority, can give the impression that they're taking a heroic stand on a moral issue without taking any risks. They do not think of the catastrophe their posturing will unleash on poor communities and the wildlife they pretend to care so much about — or at least one hopes they haven't thought of it, for if they have, their grandstanding is truly unforgivable.

Much of the popular appetite for a ban on the importation of hunting trophies arose in 2015, when a Zimbabwean lion called Cecil was killed at the hands of an American trophy hunter. When reports of this event emerged, the world went mad. Soon, every news outlet was fixated on the incident, and thousands of social media posts expressed yearning for the hunter's death. But in fact, lions live eight to ten years in the wild, and Cecil was thirteen. He was likely months away from a very unpleasant death either by starvation or a territory feud with another lion. Instead, fortunately for Cecil, a rich dentist from Minnesota threw 50,000 US dollars into the local economy in Zimbabwe so that he could give this creature a better ending than it ever could have hoped for. The television host Piers Morgan took to the TV screen to shout, completely falsely, that Cecil the lion "was skinned alive!" When Morgan's television guest expressed doubt about this account, Morgan then snapped, "Well you don't know anything about it then!" But it was Morgan who was clearly ignorant of the facts.

Piers Morgan's ignorance illustrates perhaps the worst aspect of our public discussion on trophy hunting: most people are not even opining any-more — however ignorantly — for they have resorted to purely *emoting*. And now, in our ridiculously bureaucratic regime, a combination of shallow, ill-informed opinions and confused emotions are converging at the level of executive power, and consequently we may soon see an array of legisla-tion across the world prohibiting sportsmen from bringing home their hunting memorabilia. This, of course, will undercut the trophy hunting world, paving the way to the kind of foreseeable wildlife and conservation tragedies to which I have alluded.

The bizarre thing is that we have a living case from which we could, if we were prepared to cogi-tate for five minutes, make our judgements on such sporting activities. Since the 2004 ban on hunt-ing with hounds in Britain, the fox, the hare, and increasingly the red deer, have gone from being respected quarry species to mere agricultural pests. For the fox and hare, it is now open season all year round, with urban hobby shooters driving into the countryside to devastate wildlife and post their achievements on their social media accounts. Tony Blair's Hunting Act 2004 has been nothing short of a catastrophe for wildlife in the UK.

In *Rural Wrongs*, Charlie Pye-Smith amply demon-strates that Blair's hunting ban has made life vastly worse both for wildlife and for rural communities throughout Britain, and yet UK politicians are currently looking for ways not only to 'tighten the hunting ban,' but extend this kind of legislative foolishness to the rest of the world with their attack on trophy hunting.

Whilst Pye-Smith's focus is that of hunting's relationship to wildlife welfare in Britain, towards the end of his book he raises the issue of trophy hunting's future:

> In the deeply impoverished part of Zimbabwe where I spent most of my time, profits from trophy hunting had enabled villagers to build classrooms and health clinics, hire teachers and nurses and establish income-generating projects like grinding mills. Instead of seeing wild animals like elephants and lions as a threat to their survival and killing them, as they did in the days before they could benefit from trophy hunting, they were now protecting them.[5]

Pye-Smith also records that Prof. Amy Dickman, Director of Oxford University's Wildlife Conservation Research Unit (WildCRU), and Prof. Adam Hart, University of Gloucestershire Professor of Science Communication, analysed all 118 statements by UK parliamentary members on the Hunting Trophies Bill during one of the longer 2023 chamber debates on the topic. These two researchers found that of the 118 statements, 85 were either false or misleading. And that number includes all nine statements by Sir Roger Gale, Conservative MP, who during the debate compared hunting to paedophilia.[6] Since then, a host of celebrities—including Lorraine Kelly, Ricky Gervais, Joanna Lumley, Boy George, and Kate Moss—have signalled their virtue

---

[5] Pye-Smith, *Rural Wrongs*, 79.
[6] Ibid., 80.

by publicly condemning trophy hunting, without a single one addressing the many arguments in its favour advanced by both professional conservationists and the developing communities that are foremost beneficiaries of the sport.

I naturally focus on this issue because, as a sportsman, it affects me personally. Undergoing the slow and arduous training in order to stalk deer humanely and responsibly in the UK was a life-transforming process. I have travelled to South Africa to hunt kudu and black wildebeest, where I have enjoyed some of the most wonderful experiences of my life; in the coming years I plan to hunt wild boar in central Europe. Hunting with a rifle is a considerable skill and such sporting pursuits have long been at the heart of our culture and the ways we renew the natural covenant with our landscapes. But really, the attack on trophy hunting is just one of a number of examples that reveal the true character of the regime under which we are all forced to toil in the civilisational unravelling that is late modernity.

It is typical for conservative-minded people to talk about the ongoing 'culture war' and how to win it. There *is* indeed a culture war, but much of that war is surface-level theatre that expresses a much deeper struggle, one of a managerial take-over of every aspect of our lives for the sake of intensifying centralised political control. And Britons, despite their tradition of national liberties, have recently grown accustomed to the admixture of managerial totalitarianism and managerial authoritarianism which all long-established political parties in the country seem committed to perpetuating.

In recent years, the difference between the UK's leading parties has been one only of *style*, not of ideology or methodology. They have all belonged to the same paradigm of managerial politics and emotional manipulation of the masses. Trophy hunting is enjoyed by a tiny number of people. There is obviously no point in wasting parliamentary time on bills that concern such a trivial population with such a niche hobby. So why do it? The answer is that the purpose of such bills is not what our regime claims it to be. The purpose is that of prolonging the appearance of moral rectitude among the political class while simultaneously passing legislation that creates precedents for future, wider-scoping legislation that will expand centralised control. What we probably need—though it would be extremely painful—is regime collapse. It may be the only way out. But for the time being, if you're standing at the sidelines applauding such bills, then whoever you are, you're just a turkey voting for Christmas.

# 7

# REWILDING
# AND THE FUTURE

'REWILDING,' THE INITIATIVE TO
turn areas of farmland into wilderness and
to release extirpated species back into established nature reserves, is currently very fashionable.
The objective is to restore ecosystems and reverse
biodiversity decline by letting wildlife and natural processes reclaim areas whilst simultaneously
reducing human management.

In 2022, a small herd of European bison was
released in Kent's West Blean and Thornden Woods,
South East England. Bison, which have not been
present in Britain for several thousand years, once
again roam in one of the few 'wild' places left in
these isles. For decades there has also been talk of
releasing Eurasian lynxes across the British Isles
(which died out here in the early Middle Ages) and
wolves in the Scottish Highlands (the last Highland
wolf having been hunted down and killed in 1680
by the famous Jacobite nobleman Sir Ewen Cameron
of Lochiel, 17th Chief of Clan Cameron).

Rewilding projects are underway across the world,
but they are especially common in Europe. It is happening in various places across the continent: the
Oder Delta in Germany, the Greater Côa Valley in
Portugal, the Central Apennines in Italy, the Oost-
vaardersplassen nature reserve in the Netherlands,
and in many other areas. Currently, good work is
being done to prevent illegal logging in Romania,
home to two-thirds of Europe's old temperate forests.

Half of Romania's forestry production sadly comes from this unlawful activity by what is known as the 'timber mafia,' but there are nonetheless excellent initiatives to conserve the unique wild habitats of the Carpathians, the Danube Delta, and the vast forests that cover the country. Romania is important due to its enormous, ancient forests and the astonishing number of large mammals — Carpathian lynx, grey wolf, European jackal, brown bear, chamois, bison, red deer, and others — that are found in impressive numbers there. Fortunately, many rewilders have their eyes on Romania and hope to protect it from further market-driven devastation.

Here in England, at Knepp Wildland in West Sussex, Sir Charles Burrell, 10th Baronet, has overseen a rewilding experiment on 3,500 acres that has become a refuge for a remarkable abundance of turtle doves, different species of bat, various kinds of snake, a thriving population of nightingales, and the first wild white storks that England has seen for six centuries. Knepp has various deer grazing on its land — red, fallow, and roe — to which have been added free-roaming herds of English longhorn cattle, Exmoor ponies, and Tamworth pigs as proxies for the aurochs (prehistoric undomesticated cattle), tarpan horses, and wild boar that long ago roamed British woods and scrubland. Knepp has also become a haven for rare birds of prey such as long-eared owls, hobbies, and peregrine falcons. Importantly, it is a sanctuary for many insects that are threatened due to modern, industrialised farming methods, which use herbicides and pesticides that cause grave damage to the whole natural world. At Knepp, the very rare Emperor butterfly and Vagrant Emperor dragonfly can now easily be seen.

Knepp is a working livestock farm and there is much demand for the meat it produces. But there, the attitude to farming is different to the industrial livestock farming to which we've widely grown accustomed. Thus, rewilding and farming have been brought together in an extraordinary and creative way, showing that these different approaches to the landscape need not be in antagonism, and can even become complementary aspects of a single farming enterprise. To many who are rightly worried about our dangerously depleted topsoil, wildlife destruction, and biodiversity decline, Knepp has pioneered what may be the future of livestock farming and land management.

Knepp is of considerable importance because hitherto rewilding and farming *have* in general been seen to be in tension. For example, many rewilders who wish to release large predators like lynx and wolf into the countryside must face farmers whose livelihoods rely on the survival and health of their lambs and calves. Furthermore, many farmers simply feel that the whole rewilding movement calls into question their long and difficult work of cultivating the landscape into a dependable source of food.

Some commentators have claimed that rewilders see humankind and human culture as fundamentally separate from the natural world. Environmental historian Prof. Dolly Jørgensen has remarked that rewilding "seeks to erase human history and involvement with the land and flora and fauna. Such an attempted split between nature and culture may prove unproductive and even harmful." [1] This dichotomy between nature and culture is one that recurs in the modern mind, and is likely the consequence of a three-century-old revolutionary process of replacing historically conditioned, contextual, embodied man — existent in families, local

---

[1] Dolly Jørgensen, "Rethinking rewilding" in *Geoforum*, vol. 65 (October 2015), 482–88.

communities, and nations — with the abstract, universal 'Man,' whose rights can be codified, purposes commodified, and desires satisfied by emancipation from concrete reality.

Be that as it may, my own knee-jerk instinct is that of enthusiasm for the rise of rewilding. As a young boy, I recall seeing masses of butterflies — red admirals, peacocks, tortoise shells, cabbage whites, common blues, and others — every time I stepped out for a summer walk. Now, I am lucky if I see one red admiral butterfly all summer. I am deeply worried about the future of wild creatures as well as the countryside that we share with them. The dual scourges of urban growth and industrialised farming are putting at risk the world which is meant to be first and foremost a home and a source of meaning before it is a 'resource.'

Counterintuitively perhaps, it was my interest in wildlife and conservation that, besides my fondness for being outdoors, got me into hunting. Hunting with hounds in particular entails a real respect for the quarry-species that is hunted, the hunt calendar being organised in part to procure the thriving of that species. I have spent much time learning to hunt with a firearm, which is a considerable and admirable skill, but I nonetheless acknowledge that one problem with the shift away from traditional methods of hunting with hounds is the absence of *the chase*. This means that large herds or crowded populations of a particular quarry are not broken up and dispersed for the health and flourishing of the species — as they would regularly be if they had many predators living alongside them in the wild — ultimately leading to increased malnutrition and disease (as well as the kind of territorial grazing that weakens biodiversity). Moreover, hounds — like wolves — will naturally isolate and run down weak

or sick quarry, and thereby protect the species from
infection. Firearms, on the other hand, do not dis-
criminate in this way.

One of England's great conservation success stories is that of the red deer of Exmoor. The red deer
there numbered around seventy by 1855. That year,
the Devon and Somerset Staghounds (DSSH) were
founded. By 1870, through careful management by
the pack, the deer reached around a thousand in
number. Today, due to the hard work of the DSSH,
for which they have been so poorly thanked by the
UK's hopeless political class, the red deer of Exmoor
number around 3,500, and large herds have spread
west and also east to the Quantock Hills, where
staghound packs have also been established to manage the herds. Of course, those who ideologically
oppose hunting with hounds ignore such cases.

Rewilding has already been coupled with hunting in the UK, as deer stalkers have been brought
into areas of Scotland to turn large numbers of red
deer into venison, to give newly planted evergreen
woodland a chance to mature. And it is not only
in the British Isles that there have been conservation successes brought about by hunting, as well
as disaster to conservation caused by unregulated,
illegal poaching. As noted previously in this volume,
across much of Africa I have witnessed how wildlife
has been well-managed, and nature reserves both
protected and expanded, due to big game hunting
as well as the establishment of infrastructures to
guard more animals from poachers.

The world, before it is a resource to be mined,
is a gift to be cared for. It is therefore regrettable
that the 'green movement' has been appropriated
by opportunists who see the world wholly as a 'sustainable resource' and 'renewable commodity.' These
managerial toerags have teamed up with those on the

extreme Left who see mankind as a disease in the
world, a parasite that does nothing but take, thereby
corrupting the health of the planet (a planet that
would be better off, they hold, without us). These two
ideological currents seem at odds, with one seeking
to commodify the earth and the other seeking to
free the earth from those who would subordinate it
to pure use. The former, however, sees population
growth to be a threat to the sustainability of the
earth as a limited resource, and so instinctively
sympathises with the misanthropy of the latter.
Thus, together these two currents have allied the
'green' agenda with an aggressive population control ideology. This population control ideology long
predates the 'green' movement with which it is now
mingled, having a pedigree that includes Malthu-
sianism and the nineteenth century eugenics movement. Today, most of those at the forefront of global
'green' initiatives hold to a worldview that comprises
an admixture of these ideological approaches. And
they see the success of their endeavours to require
a dramatically reduced human population that is
severed from the natural world, a world which they
claim would thrive if only left alone by us.

Viewing 'green' as a category of the Left, too many
conservative-minded people have conceded all the
political and cultural territory concerning nature
conservation to their adversaries, and now have
little to say on the topic. The exceptions are found
only among some especially expansive thinkers like
Roger Scruton and Paul Kingsnorth.[2]

Conservative-minded folk have largely failed to
fight for their proper place as the *true* green-warriors,

---

[2] See Roger Scruton, *Green Philosophy: How to Think Seriously About
the Planet* (London: Atlantic Books, 2012); Paul Kingsnorth,
*Confessions of a Recovering Environmentalist* (London: Faber & Faber,
2017).

and they have been routinely embarrassed to pro-
pose the simple conservation activities that actually
work — localist initiatives like park management,
tree-planting, gardening, smallholding, pickling,
beekeeping, and hunting. Having abandoned the
'green movement' to the Left, old-fashioned conservatives are instinctively suspicious of internationally
coordinated rewilding projects. Anything advanced
in defence of the world that we inhabit, they reason,
must be driven by motives incompatible with their
worldview, for such enterprises are now entirely in
the hands of their enemy. They may not be wrong
to have such suspicions, but the proper response
should be that of forming a truly *conservative* 'green
movement,' not stepping out of the conservation
conversation altogether.

It is undeniable that enthusiasm for rewilding
has coincided with the rise of a certain vision of
mankind as a 'problem' to be solved, rather than
the summit of creation to be celebrated. It is easy
to see why this enthusiasm for rewilding has arisen
alongside such a misanthropic vision, given the
extensive available evidence of our poor ecological
stewardship. In turn, many believe that we must
re-create the world as if we had never been in it.
We must undo the cultivated world and recover the
wild world. We can then finally drive a sharp wedge
between man and nature. Man will finally leave
nature alone, being confined to his carbon-neutral
cities where, when feeling starved of the natural
world he used to inhabit, he may visit its substitute
in virtual reality. In this progressivist future of our
managerial masters, interaction with the natural
world found in good farming will have been rendered unnecessary as we grow our food in colossal
polytunnels in a well-irrigated Sahara, planted and
harvested by robots. Meat, for those barbarians who

still consume it, will be grown from protein cells in test tubes and delivered in aluminium pouches by drones as we all conduct our digital work from home. Given that the top 1 percent of the world's rich who own 40 percent of the world's wealth have hugely invested in the technology to move us onto test tube meat and insect-based proteins, such a food industry now seems inevitable.[3] As we increasingly become unwell on our new diet and the vast amount of radiation and chemicals needed to run our technologized world—and perhaps are hit by the occasional Chinese bioweapon—we shall routinely have to turn to the pharmaceuticals that are owned by (guess who!) that same 1 percent. We might avoid this nightmare, of course, by unplugging ourselves, moving out of our urban apartments, and then smallholding on cheap, remote land—but let's be honest, we would probably all choose comfort, bug food, and illness instead. And fortunately for our overlords, such a trajectory would likely lead to the reduced, moderately wealthy population that they believe both the earth and the market so desperately need.

In this dystopia, in which a reduced human population of technologized *chosen* lives in a parallel urban world to the natural one from which it has been utterly sundered, man will have achieved the antithesis of what he was always supposed to do, namely carefully turn this hostile world into a home. Having rejected the imperative to make a home out of this world, man will have fled the world

---

[3] See Damian Carrington, "No-kill, lab-grown meat to go on sale for first time," *The Guardian*, December 1, 2020, https://www.theguardian.com/environment/2020/dec/02/no-kill-lab-grown-meat-to-go-on-sale-for-first-time; Richard Godwin, "If we want to save the planet, the future of food is insects," *The Guardian*, May 8, 2021, https://www.theguardian.com/food/2021/may/08/if-we-want-to-save-the-planet-the-future-of-food-is-insects.

altogether to enter a simulated world of his own
making. Of course, that virtual world, in which
he has made a virtual home, will reflect his heart
from which it has come, and there is nothing darker
than the heart of man once he has fled his purpose.

It worries me that rewilding harmonises so well
with the construction of this Brave New World. It
brings me no joy to reflect so pessimistically. As
stated, rewilding is an enterprise with which I have
instinctive sympathy. It could mark the beginnings
of an escape from a vision of the world as something to be commodified rather than conserved
and cherished. Rewilding could help to move us
out of the conception of nature as a "torture chamber," as Goethe characterized modernity's view, and
return us to our ancestors' vision of the natural
world—that is, a theophanic mystery whose fruits
sustain our lives.

I venture to suggest that rewilding is something
that conservative-minded people should make their
own, and thereby rescue this fashionable initiative
from the sinister ideological motives by which in
part it is being shaped. Greater involvement by such
people requires, as a fundamental prerequisite, the
courage to claim that man has a role as steward
and guardian over the natural world, of which
he is an inseparable part. Restoring our proper
relationship with the natural world, it must be
asserted, does not entail a retreat from nature but
a renewed immersion in its mystery and a humble
submission to its laws.

The ideologues who believe that mankind needs
to enter into a completely different mode of life may
not be wrong, they may only be mistaken about
what shape that change must take. Rather than a
globalised, technologized, urbanised, sterile, population of managers, ordering about computerised

proxy-workers in a virtual world, perhaps we need to restore a local, simple, domestic, less-industrialised, more *natural* way of life, that privileges the flourishing of humans, of the world we inhabit, and of the creatures we share it with, over endless productivity and consumption. That, however, will require rescuing the 'green movement' from misanthropic progressivists, the globalist oligarchs who crave power, and, importantly, the phoney 'conservatives' who celebrate the market as the highest possible good.

# 8

# NATURE RED IN TOOTH
# AND CLAW

BOUT FIFTEEN YEARS AGO, I
was out in the woods for a late afternoon
ramble with my spaniel Monty, and I lost
my bearings. It got darker, and I realized that the
footpath from which I'd foolishly strayed would soon
be invisible to me in the twilight, even if it were
only a few yards away. This emerald entanglement of
buzzing life where I'd been ambling with awe rapidly
transformed into a murky, obscure, creaking maze of
threatening shapes and biotic tripwires. I eventually
escaped after an hour of wandering—which was
enough to learn something new about the woods.

I continue to wander in the woods often. In those
arboreal labyrinths I encounter the God who, as the
Book of Genesis puts it, "looked upon everything
that He had made and saw that it was very good."
The woods have an ability to draw me into ecstasy,
and I commonly experience, entranced like a gawp-
ing idiot in those secret chantries under leafy vaults,
a state of hyper-awareness that I am enclosed by a
matrix of living reality in immeasurable manifes-
tations, overlapping, interdepending, and conjoining
in a veritable convergence of pure vitality. The distinction between myself and the cosmos of which I
am a part becomes blurred in such moments, and
the separateness of things becomes a way by which
to grasp their co-extensiveness. Invariably, at these
moments, an ephemeral tranquillity enters the depth
of my soul which is totally incommunicable. And

yet, I have not forgotten that with the withdrawal of light that bequeaths life to that viridescent realm, the woods change to terrorise the mind.

The woodland that was revealed to me on that evening of confused wandering is, I am told, the permanent condition of unmanaged rainforests around the world. Indeed, I recall something of this from when, years ago, I crossed part of the Nepalese Chitwan rainforest on the back of an elephant. A hairy caterpillar fell from a branch overhead and landed on my arm, immediately rolling off and leaving a thick red stripe on my skin where whatever its toxic stubbles had left behind continued to irritate me for days. I became cognisant of the fact that I was surrounded by creepy-crawlies that are less than benign. Nature remains, in the immortal words of Lord Tennyson, "red in tooth and claw."

A friend of mine, an officer in the British Army, was once stationed in Brunei for two years. After he returned, he remarked to me that the rainforest out there is *not* beautiful. It is thorny and tangled, humid and pestilent, dark and suffocating, and the animals do not call to each other but screech and fight in hidden hollows among the canopies. The locals, he said, are terrified of the rainforest and prefer to remain in concrete apartment blocks, from which they rarely venture unless forced by necessity. They believe, he explained, that the rainforest is where demons live.

As my friend spoke, I was reminded of the scene in 1986 film *The Mission*, in which Fr Gabriel—the Jesuit priest brilliantly portrayed by Jeremy Irons—is told by one of the little Amerindian boys that he doesn't want to return to the rainforest. When Fr Gabriel translates to Cardinal Altamirano who is with him what the child said, the Cardinal asks why the boy doesn't want to go back into the forest, to which Fr Gabriel replies, "He says that the devil lives there."

My friend told me of a Bruneian soldier who became separated from his squadron in the rainforest, and after many days of searching, any hope of finding him was abandoned. He appeared, though, downstream weeks later—desperately weak but alive—and was brought back to the barracks. Following much questioning on how he had survived, the soldier eventually explained: after a couple of days, a female *jinni*—a spirit, according to Islamic tradition—appeared to him and told him that she could keep him alive only if he would marry her. He refused. Later, when he was on the brink of death by starvation, the jinni appeared again and made her request once more. This time he agreed, and she sustained him over the ensuing weeks until he made his way out of the forest. The man said to his officers that he couldn't forgive himself for his decision to enter this unholy union with the spirit, but in the barracks he was often found alone talking with his otherworldly spouse—whom only he could see. Eventually, he was dismissed from the military and soon after took his own life.

Succubi and incubi appear in Christian demonology, and similar phenomena are also found in the traditional stories of the West. In the folk ballad "King Henry," first written down in the 1790s and catalogued by Vaughan Williams in the early twentieth century, a Scottish king returns from a day's hunting only to find his banquet interrupted by a female demon. His friends and courtiers flee, leaving the king alone with the demoness in his hunting lodge's hall. She commands him to kill his horse, greyhounds, and goshawks, that she may eat them. He obeys and she gorges. She then drinks the king's wine and tells him to make a bed, that the two of them may lie down together:

Take off your clothes now King Henry
And lie down by my side
Now swear, now swear you King Henry
To take me for your bride.

Oh God forbid, says King Henry,
That ever the like betide,
That ever a fiend that comes from hell
Should stretch down by my side.

When King Henry wakes up in the morrow, the demoness is lying next to him but now she is transformed into "The fairest lady that ever was seen," as the song says.

There are many ways to interpret this song, and no doubt most interpretations are correct — that's how these songs work. But one interpretation is that having succumbed to the demonic presence and its demands, the king awoke in the morn to find that he liked his new servitude, and thus was well and truly ensnared. He had gone out hunting in the wild, and by morning found himself imprisoned by its powers.

The ballad of King Henry may be based on another, older, and much longer song entitled "The Marriage of Sir Gawain." The tale of the song is that the knight-errant Sir Gawain is forced by King Arthur into a marriage with a very ugly and accursed woman whom the king has met in a wooded glade. But she is eventually freed from her curse by Gawain and transforms into a beautiful young lady. In this tale, the hag is drawn from nature and becomes beautiful by her induction into the courtly and civilised life of the knightly fellowship. Of course, in the widely loved poem *Sir Gawain and the Green Knight*, Gawain's experiences are filled with bewitchments and enchantments. And again, in that poem it is nature that is cursed.

*Sir Gawain and the Green Knight* begins with the Christmas celebration of King Arthur and his knights, a feast which is disturbed by the Green Knight who is the personification of raw nature. He is nature embodied, who, when slain by Sir Gawain, is immediately reanimated and challenges the young knight. Thereafter, it is in the wild that Gawain is tested. Then he finds himself at the castle of a lord who only feels fully himself when out in the wilderness, into which he rides with the hunt every day to enjoy the thrill of the chase, leaving Gawain in the company of his lady who tests both Gawain's courtesy and purity. Finally, Gawain goes to the Green Chapel, literally nature's hallowed sanctuary, where he must face the Green Knight and face his death. He survives, but he loses his honour—at least in his own eyes. At each stage, nature is presented as hostile, dangerous, bloody, deceiving, and disordered.

In the early centuries of the Church's life, the desert fathers and the great ascetics of the Celtic tradition ventured out into the wilderness to contend with demons. Our artistic tradition testifies to this spiritual heritage, with the Temptation of St Anthony being an especially loved topic among the great masters of the Renaissance (and among their works on this theme, there is nothing that equals Hieronymus Bosch's *Triptych of Temptation of St Anthony*). This leads me to wonder whether talk of 'rewilding Christianity,' popularised by writers such as Martin Shaw and Paul Kingsnorth—both of whom I admire, I hasten to add—may be just as romantic as the popular appetite for rewilding itself. Man, it must be observed, is always falling into some type of neo-primitivism. This is an error on which Rousseau capitalised, and which is especially tempting in our age, when we're losing our grip on technology and growing unsure of whether technologies serve us or we serve them.

Hieronymus Bosch, *The Temptation of Saint Anthony*, ca. 1500

This is where I suspect Kingsnorth in particular has misconstrued the cosmic pilgrimage of the baptised. I was once fortunate enough to hear him speak at an event in London, at which he delivered what I can only describe as a first-class sermon on the Christian story of salvation. But a major theme of his talk was that of the *setting* into which man was placed at the moment of his creation: Eden. Our proper home, Kingsnorth told his audience, is where the plants and the animals are—that is, the wild. But he overlooks the fact that man is so created with an accompanying commandment to cultivate Eden that it may be a garden harmonious and pleasing to God, as Holy Scripture says: "The Lord God took the man and put him in the garden of Eden *to till it and keep it.*"

Our technologically driven alienation undoubtedly marks a colossal spiritual danger, but that should not cause us to lose sight of an important truth: man actuates his nature through civilisation and not by returning to the wild. To paraphrase Edmund Burke: civilisation *is* man's nature. Nature is not the realm of our redemption, and thus it needs to be permeated by grace, a supernatural principle which must be extended to all that baptised man touches—including the wild. In fact, in the Christian narrative, all nature was placed under the jurisdiction of the devil following man's fall from grace. The wilderness is not where the sanctuary is found but likely where a hive of demons awaits. And as much as it troubles a countryside bumpkin like me to acknowledge it, the Christian must accept that whilst his origins are in the garden, his final glorification is in the city, the New Jerusalem. Heaven is urban, where perfect urbanism and perfect urbanity converge. That doesn't mean that heaven is a celestial version of modern London; in fact, I expect it's more like a transfigured Stow-on-the-Wold.

The old countryside landscapes of Europe are what you get once you've exorcised the wilderness of its hellish chaos and transformed it into a reliable source of food and clothing, and more importantly, a real home for civilised man. Rejecting the technologized, mechanistic, materialistic anti-civilisation of late modernity that constantly stifles the human spirit need not mean embracing a sentimental primitivism. In my view, it should mean retrieving Christendom.

Our ancestors knew nature, and they thought it was frightening. We also intuit that it's frightening, which is why we're fleeing nature through technologies that un-anchor the 'self' from the body, and by extension from the natural world altogether. But the way to deal with the terror of nature, which is a very real terror, is neither to romanticise it nor run from it. Rather, like the desert fathers, we must contend with nature and all who linger in its twisted paths, that it may be redeemed.

In fact, I would go further and suggest that the best way to contend with the terror of nature is—like the Benedictine monks of old whom Kingsnorth accuses of wrongly "taming" Christianity—that of transforming raw nature into barley fields, olive groves, and vineyards.[4] Nature is not 'the environment'—some mass of things out there—but a reality contiguous with whatever we are, on which we must imprint our presence. That is what it is to till and keep the garden.

Just as we must *personalise* the chaos of our human nature, and thereby emerge as persons, that we may be pleasing to God and neighbour, so too can all that we touch be so converted. This is likely why nature is so terrifying to us: all its horror—the poisons, the

---

[4] See Paul Kingsnorth, "A Wild Christianity," *First Things*, March 1, 2023, https://www.firstthings.com/article/2023/03/a-wild-christianity.

thorns, the parasites, the tearing of flesh — is fully present in distilled form in the human heart. The only way to survive such darkness in the heart is arduously to tame it for the sake of others, and we rightly desire to extend that noble impulse to any part of the world we wish to inhabit. The problem, then, is *not* that impulse. Rather, it is the corruption of that impulse in late modernity, an epoch that has conflated tilling with dominating, cultivation with consumption, and the sanctified soul with the 'authentic self.'

In recent times, a fad called 'forest bathing' has emerged among urban dwellers. This activity comprises travelling out to some woodland and, well, *being in it.* The point is calmly to sway amongst the trees in the hope of momentarily suspending one's technology- and isolation-driven anxiety, ultimately to experience the 'mental health' of an average pre-modern. And of course, only those who are sufficiently removed from nature can have such a conception of nature as a benign source of personal wellbeing.

The forest is not a place of peace; it is a dark chamber where animals hunt and are hunted, from which the sane seek refuge to huddle by the hearth. Of course, we must rediscover nature and our contiguity with it, but that will mean encountering not something consoling but a chaotic realm in need of redemption. For this reason, the hunting of quarry was always at the heart of our common culture, and that is why no activity is more threatened by both technologized urbanisation and animal-centric sentimentalism. By hunting, we rediscovered nature and ourselves as a part of it, and we did this not by syrupy feelings but by respecting nature's inner violence, simultaneously making it our own and beautifying it beyond measure — a power that is unique to our species.

# 9

# ENTERING THE
# LITTLE PLATOONS
# TO SAVE ENGLAND

I N A PARK IN THE TOWN ON WHOSE
outskirts we live, there is a garden. It is a beautiful garden, and it is there for no other purpose
than to beautify the rest of the park and the lives
of its visitors. The small trees, the plants, and the
many flowers change throughout the year, selected
to survive the seasons, being continuously tended
by a small team of middle-aged ladies and gentlemen. These people are volunteers. They do not live
near the garden, and they are unable to enjoy its
blossoms apart from during those visits to its beds
when they bestow their careful attention.

This group of volunteers, week in week out, mind
this garden for the benefit of everyone else, and
they are rarely—if ever—thanked by their count-
less beneficiaries. The garden is a true 'common
good.' It is not a 'private good,' enjoyed only by one
or few individuals. It is not a 'shared good,' that
can be divided up among a certain group, vanishing in the process. It is a common good, for the
degree to which someone enjoys the garden is not
the degree to which others don't enjoy it. And in
fact, the more one enjoys it, the more enjoyable it is
for everyone else. In this way, the garden is meta-
physically superabundant—though I don't think its
gardeners would put it quite like that. The garden
is also completely pointless. Or rather, it has no
point beyond itself. It contains within itself its own

purpose. Thus, by virtue of its uselessness, it is one
of the most important things in the town, for whilst
most things are mere *means*, this garden is an *end*.

It is increasingly typical for those who are worried about the future of their societies to talk of
a great conspiracy of the 'deep state' against the
people. Such anxious commentators, however, rarely
see that — whether there is such a thing as a 'deep
state' conspiracy or not — *they* are more likely the
problem behind their society's ills than corrupt
pin-striped politicians plotting in secret basements.
Society *is* disappearing, and it won't be salvaged by
winning arguments in the comments sections of
YouTube videos. The only way to save society is to
immerse ourselves in it for the good of everyone
else. Infinitely more counter-revolutionary than the
internet reactionary complaining about the deep
state cabal is the gardener in the park.

Unfortunately, young people do not join clubs
and associations anymore. They are content to
intensify their solipsism by associating with others only through the portal of their social media
accounts. Membership, *true* membership, by which
a community's members mingle and become part
of each other's lives, is a retreating feature of our
existence. The young internet reactionary is all
too inclined to assume that he can transform his
society, moving it towards what he thinks would
be better, and that he can do this by distancing
himself from that society and standing in judgement
over it — judgement frequently expressed in cynical
and sneering social media posts. This, however, is
to take the easy way out.

It is commonly observed by conservative-minded
people that the leftist's great sin is that of loving
humanity. Humanity is easy to love, for it demands
only an inner feeling and no more. In truth, one

ought to love one's *neighbour*, who is likely almost
unbearable. On the other hand, the internet reactionary's great sin is to bemoan the disappearance
of his civilisation whilst making little to no effort
to induct himself into what actually remains of it,
with a view to revitalising the rest. He doesn't join
the local council, or become a member of the local
historical society, or the village woodland trust, or
a bellringer for the parish, or a whipper-in for the
beagles. He thinks the real battles happen online,
whilst the *actual* society that he claims to want to
save has been abandoned by him.

Last summer, I saw, in the most striking vision,
what a vigorous society can bring about. I found
myself at a window seat on a flight back to England
from Italy. For the few hours this flight lasted, there
wasn't a single cloud in the sky. I read nothing, and
I didn't sleep a minute. I just watched as the Old
Continent passed by beneath. I admired the great
lakes of northern Italy, the colossal teeth of the Alps,
and the vast landscapes of France. As the aeroplane
flew over the north of France, however, I was aston-
ished by the sheer ugliness of the land. All the way
to the horizon, as far as the eye could see, was a
great beige grid. Rectangular field after rectangular
field, comprising one massive Excel spreadsheet of
arable industry. If I were asked to visually represent the rationalist, Napoleonic, codified modernity
that the French forced in different forms on most
of the world, I could find nothing better than the
industrialised farmlands of northern France.

Then, France was left behind, and over the
Channel we flew. My heart leapt as the white
cliffs emerged across the briny. From above, the
English countryside was a marvel to behold, especially in comparison to the unbeautiful parcels
of agricultural rationalism of moments earlier. I

suddenly understood why French novels are urban
and English novels are bucolic (apart from those of
Dickens, who gives us a solely hellish vision of city
life anyway). I gazed in wonder at the swirling fields
that followed the contours of the land, the hedgerows, the woodlands, the thickets and copses, the
canals and rivers. The English countryside, far from
a grid, was more like a great medieval tapestry, full
of colour and surprise. England's rural community,
I saw, had evaded rationalism and found sanctuary
in spontaneity.

Why was it, I thought, that England's countryside
looked this way? It is because—until recently, in
any case—we have not treated our landscape as a
mere provider of food only, but as the guardian of
a way of life. Our coverts are filled with gamebirds
that we shoot for sport and gobble at Christmas.
Foxes and hares, the traditional quarry of those
who hunt with hounds, also need these hideouts to
escape the pack and keep the chase sporting. The
canals and rivers are lined with anglers in fair
weather, a rare climatic occurrence treated with
reverence by the English. The woodlands are full
of deer (more prevalent today in Britain than at
any time in recorded history), whose venison is
treasured throughout the land. Ramblers and hikers
have pressed for more footpaths, and the countryside
is deemed a good—a *common good*—for all those who
like to visit and rediscover that they are not, after
all, robots. Farmers are rightly jealous of their lands,
and yet they routinely do their part in maintaining
the footpaths and bridleways, because they know
better than anyone that England's countryside and
its inherited culture are indivisible.

In short, rural England looks the way it does due
to the English genius for institution-building. Yes,
there are the grand institutions like the monarchy,

the two houses of Parliament, the Inns of Court, and so forth. But there are also the "little platoons," as Burke's phrase goes: all those little societies, clubs, trusts, associations, communities, and unions that make up English society. The farms, the hunts, the shoots, the fisheries, the ramblers' associations, the countryside trusts, and all the little bottom-up, organic 'platoons' of membership, which are so normal to the English, have made their land the spectacle that it is.

On the Continent, it is common for people to live in apartment blocks at the centres of cities and large towns. Many of these buildings' apartments are almost palatial, and I have enjoyed generous hospitality in many of them during my travels. Continental Europeans do not seem to mind living close to one another, or knowing more than just the names of their neighbours. It is a moral defect of the English that they so keenly guard their privacy. (No doubt this trait comes from our inordinate affection for bourgeois culture, and our egalitarian discomfort with public, aristocratic culture—which is just another way of saying, our *envy*.) Every Englishman wants his own house with its own garden and a fence going all the way round—a cheap substitute for the moat that he'd prefer. Our beautiful countryside is always, therefore, under threat, as the sprawling suburbs of urban centres increasingly grow with each man insisting on keeping his own 'castle.'

The English have negotiated a way of maintaining the privacy that they hold sacred, and simultaneously preventing the complete atomisation of society: they have emphasised civil association. The English genius for institution-building is what has conserved the English nation, rather than allowing it to become a mere island of detached houses with each household declaring itself a nation in its own right. England has survived by becoming a land of little platoons, communities of people who bind themselves to one another whilst respecting the privacy that they've come to enjoy. This has been, in some ways, a huge achievement. The outcome, though, entails that if the platoons die out, so does England.

The lack of interest found among the young in joining and perpetuating such 'platoons,' then, is very worrying. That modern phenomenon, alongside the volume of immigrants coming to England who have little interest in its culture and history, or in adopting the ways of life that have made England what it is, may mean that what is left of real England will soon be snuffed out. If Blighty *can* be salvaged, that will not come about by accruing a certain number of 'likes' on Facebook or squabbling in a YouTube comments box. Those who long to restore our society and lay claim to our cultural inheritance must step into the square and make it their own. There is no other way.

# 10

# HIKING AND THE BURKEAN CONTRACT

I N TWILIGHT'S INFANCY, AS THE sun set, the field through which my dog and I passed was bathed in the gold that broke through the clouds, a light that reflected as silver-blue off the burned ears atop the long grass. The hills rolled into the distance where a train raced through the otherwise peaceful country. Little copses and overgrown hedgerows rang with the squawks of squabbling rooks and jackdaws. My dog stood entranced, fixed on a hare at the other end of the field that he knew he'd never catch. Fat wood pigeons cooed in the treetops of the elms and oaks, which danced in the gentle wind to the sounds of the surrounding creatures.

I looked around, and I saw that the world was *gift*. There are complex metaphysical arguments from contingency by which one can argue that the proper way to see the world is through the prism of *Giver*, *gift*, and *recipient*. To grasp the structure of a satisfying philosophical case, however, is quite different to responding to the world as gift with the appropriate affectivity. One thing is to know that the world is gift, another thing is to *feel* gratitude in the reception of it.

Whilst there is a primary, ontological sense by which the world we inhabit can be understood as *gift*, there is also an historical sense. This latter sense, it seems to me, is of the utmost importance not only for developing the proper affectivity to

respond appropriately to the world, but also that
one may in steps come to see the reasonableness of
the metaphysical case.

My dog and I, on our evening hike, making our
way across that field, stopped, and looked out. I
intentionally attended to the world revealed before
me. Then, having gazed upon those tawny hills that
flanked the vale which ran to the retreating sun, I
discerned the presence of *the holy Lamb of God on England's
pleasant pastures seen.* This great landscape, however,
gave way to the earth under my boots. I looked at
the ground, and I beheld an astonishing spectacle.

The field itself, to which I had given so little attention, was a technicoloured marvel. Greens, lilacs,
oranges, yellows, blues, pinks, all unfolded below. In
the square foot at which I alone stared, there must
have been over fifty grass species. The great panorama of which I was a part disappeared from my
mind's eye as I gaped with amazement at the kalei-
doscopic wonder which bended to my trampling bulk.

This vision was not merely a miracle of nature, but
of art. From the seventeenth century onwards, farmers used grass manuals to work out which grasses
could be grown together, and how to make the
most nutritious and diverse meadows for the perfect
livestock pasture. This breath-taking biodiversity at
which I gawked was the product of human ingenuity
down the centuries. The field over which I all too
mindlessly wandered was pregnant with the toil and
sweat of generations. The thought that our spawn
might come and fail to see what I saw, and build
some monstrous shopping centre over this meadow
where rabbits played and jays bickered, was a dark
imagining sufficient to break my heart.

The feelings that accompany experiences of this
kind are those which are necessary to move the
intellect, that one may see oneself not as an isolated

being that has been dropped into the void and is soon to expire. Rather, one sees oneself as a life in a great *stream of life*, emerging out of the story of one's ancestors and wider community, in turn to be perpetuated through the rising of one's progeny, whose flourishing will be causally related to one's own. One sees, but more importantly one *feels*, that the world is bestowed by the great council of the dead who have a say in the discussion of the living, we ephemeral beings who are the beneficiaries of ancient labour. We enjoy what we have because when we didn't exist, we were nonetheless kept in mind by those who have ceased to wander here below, and that spiritual assembly now demands that we think of those yet to come.

This, in the end, is the problem with the Burkean Contract, which is no contract at all, but a moral covenant between the dead, the living, and the unborn. In Burke's own words:

> [Society is] a partnership in every virtue and in all perfection. As the ends of such a partnership cannot be obtained in many generations, it becomes a partnership not only between those who are living, but between those who are living, those who are dead, and those who are to be born. Each contract of each particular state is but a clause in the great primeval contract of eternal society... connecting the visible and invisible world.[1]

It is very difficult to argue for the Burkean Contract. If one sees oneself as a morally isolated, radical individual for whom history means nothing and for whom nothing is owed to the future, no amount

---

[1] Edmund Burke, *Reflections on the Revolution in France* (London: Penguin Books, 1986), 194.

of disputation will let in the light. The Burkean
Contract, it seems to me, denotes a mystery, the
true meaning of which is only unveiled when the
right feelings are conjured up within by the experience of reality as *gift*.

People exclusively buy furniture now rather than
inherit it. They deem the fashions of the past to
belong to the past, and they do not feel that the
past belongs to them. Into the skip the furniture
therefore goes. Each generation believes that it is
starting from scratch, and must surround itself
with the disposable rubbish that testifies to such
an erroneous belief. (The remarkable success of Ikea
depends on this unspoken conviction held by nearly
all in the West.) Inherited things and old things
are didactic. They sit there in a corner, or silently
cradle one's bottom, and mutely teach us that the
past is present, and that *conserved things* bestow value.

Can the feelings necessary to grasp the Burkean
Contract be taught? I think they can. But they
cannot be easily taught, it seems to me, through
propositional pronouncements. Rather, the fostering
of these feelings begins with story-telling, especially
of national legends, fairy tales, and fables. Such
feelings can also be fostered through traditional
folk music, listening to which should in turn allow
for some sensitivity to the great achievements of
classical music, and Vaughan Williams provides
wonderful transitionary pieces. Plays, recitals, and
dances are all necessary. Sports and hobbies supple-
ment this induction into a meaningful life. Local
fairs and visits to places of historical importance
are essential too. More serious literature can be
introduced. Finally, poetry. The reason why the
poet has always had a quasi-mystical status in our
civilisation is because he is the true teacher of feelings. We have always known that feelings can be

taught, and that failure to teach feelings will have a catastrophic effect on our civilisation. Hence, we have always known that the poet must be esteemed.

Corresponding to the teachability of feelings is the notion that they can be untaught.[2] Indeed, our entire 'pop culture' operates to undo the proper cultivation of affectivity that our civilisational inheritance would otherwise organically nurture. If we lose our capacity for the affectivity presupposed by the Burkean Contract, then we lose our civilisation altogether. Quite literally, we cease to be *a people*, and become isolated individuals. Unfeeling, solipsistic individuals are not persons, but something else.

Many conservative-minded people have unfortunately habituated the tendency to oppose rational argument to feelings, seeing their social and political opponents to be dominated by the latter. In fact, the problem we have today is not the absence of reason and the dominance of feeling, but the ascendency of bad reasoning and the supremacy of self-directed fake emotion—all enabled by an absence of real culture. What is desperately needed is an education in feelings, and that education begins with real culture and ends with signing the Burkean Contract in one's blood.

---

[2] Readers of C.S. Lewis will recall that this is a point brilliantly made in the first chapter of *The Abolition of Man* (New York: HarperCollins, 2001), 1-26.

# 11

# ON CARRYING
# A POCKETKNIFE

SINCE TIME IMMEMORIAL, MEN
have carried weapons. They have done so—
if they were *real* men—not to pick fights or
unnecessarily injure other men, but in response
to the heavy burden of walking life's path in this
world as a protector. Only a few centuries ago, a
gentleman would wear a smallsword or spadroon
just in case the need arose to defend his good name,
as well as all those who shared in that name. As
the smallsword was increasingly regulated by the
law of the land, and gentlemen relied more on
the State or, if it came to that, the courts, to settle
their affairs, gentlemen nonetheless carried canes—
around which sprang the martial art made famous
by Sherlock Holmes: Bartitsu.

G.K. Chesterton, in his autobiography, reflecting
on the unusual purchases he made on his honey-
moon, brings to the fore the desire of everyman
to fulfil the imperative to be a protector of those
whom he loves:

> It is alleged against me, and with perfect
> truth, that I stopped on the way to drink
> a glass of milk in one shop and to buy a
> revolver with cartridges in another. Some
> have seen these as singular wedding-presents
> for a bridegroom to give to himself, and if
> the bride had known less of him, I suppose
> she might have fancied that he was a suicide
> or a murderer or, worst of all, a teetotaller.

They seemed to me the most natural things
in the world. I did not buy the pistol to
murder myself—or my wife; I never was
really modern. I bought it because it was the
great adventure of my youth, with a general
notion of protecting her from the pirates
doubtless infesting the Norfolk Broads,
to which we were bound; where, after all,
there are still a suspiciously large number
of families with Danish names. I shall not
be annoyed if it is called childish; but obviously it was rather a reminiscence of boy-
hood, and not of childhood.[1]

Any normal man grows up with the fantasy firmly
lodged in his head that this world is full of pirates,
and his job is to kill them. This fantasy, in fact, is
not a fantasy at all but a myth. Like all great myths,
it recurs in every balanced psyche, and appears in
a thousand forms in every existent culture, for the
sole reason that it represents a fundamental truth.
Any man will invariably see his life, at bottom, as
a tale of loving those to whom his life is linked
and hence killing the 'pirates' that seek to frustrate
both their lives and his own.

Of course, by 'killing,' in an age in which smalls-
words and even revolvers are out of fashion, I
mean *metaphorically killing*. Clearly, the revolver that
Chesterton bought was never meant to be used, but
was purchased as a reminder of that fundamental
myth: his life would have meaning bestowed upon it
inasmuch as he accepted the responsibility to *protect*.

Being a protector, however, is just one aspect of
a much broader imperative with which every man
is faced: the imperative to be a servant. The dichot-
omising of leadership and service—a *real* dichotomy

---

[1] G.K. Chesterton, *Autobiography* (London: Hutchinson &
Co., 1937), 37.

for the pagans, as Nietzsche exhibited so well—was
so deeply undermined by the Good Shepherd who
laid down his life for his sheep, that an entire civilisation emanated from its eventual obliteration. To
lead one's family, one's business, one's parish . . . is
to place oneself at the service of a community and
put one's own flourishing in second place after those
whom one leads, a process by which one's own flourishing—paradoxically—is obtained.

These are all rather deep, and perhaps excessively
moralistic, points to be making. Allow me, therefore,
to bring things down to the mundane: pocketknives.
It is my conviction, based on innumerable experiences, that a pocketknife is an essential bit of kit for
any man who wants to be a great servant-leader. My
father has always carried a pocketknife, as I'm sure
did his father, and his father, as have my siblings,
as have I. In adulthood, rarely has a day gone by on
which I haven't reached for my pocketknife for the
small benefit of someone else. In this way, carrying
a pocketknife is itself a small act of charity.

My pocketknife, being a Victorinox (and therefore exquisitely made), is more than just a knife.
Besides the non-locking 2.8-inch blade (making it
a legal everyday-carry in the UK), it has scissors,
a bottle-opener, a can-opener, two screwdrivers, a
wire-stripper, a ballpoint pen, a toothpick, tweezers,
a hook, a nailfile, a corkscrew, and a needle (perfect for getting out splinters). My pocketknife is
extremely useful. Many a time, for example, have
friends and I found ourselves in the desperate situation—something I wouldn't wish on anyone—
of discovering that we were without a corkscrew.
Before despair engulfed us, however, I was able to
save the day with my pocketknife.

I grew up regularly witnessing how useful my
father made himself by use of his pocketknife. As

early as possible, I petitioned to have my own. At age five, my son began to do the same, so I bought for him a toy pocketknife, of which he was very proud indeed. The desire of boys to carry pocket-knives, it seems to me, is one that should be nurtured. Each time I draw it from my pocket to peel an orange for my child, or crack open a few foraged walnuts whilst out walking in the woods, or open a bottle of beer for a chum, I enjoy a glimpse of the hunter-gatherer life. That is, of the self-reliance that our ancestors knew, from which the technologization of society swiftly removed us. A pocketknife makes one more useful to others, and being at the service of others is what turns a boy into a man.

One summer, I took my wife and children camping in the West Country. On the last evening, we popped over to a shop in a nearby town and bought a bottle of wine as well as some bottles of rose lemonade for the children. We also bought marshmallows for toasting. The wine was opened with the corkscrew on my pocketknife. The lemonades were opened with the bottle-opener on my pocketknife. The marshmallows were put on sticks cut from a tree with my pocketknife, the bark of which had been cut away and the ends whittled down to a fine point—all with my pocketknife. That night we kicked back with a couple of plastic cups filled with robust Amarone and watched the children's happy faces illumined by the firelight. I can instantly recall their giggles of excitement as they toasted their marshmallows. That evening remains one of the happiest memories of my fatherhood—and it was largely made possible because I carry a pocketknife.

Many, especially on the 'internet-Right,' complain about a crisis of masculinity that is, it is claimed, corrupting the West. There is surely much truth in this view, but the causes are so far out of our control that highlighting the fact leads more to desolation than action. When one steps back and looks at the challenge before us, it is difficult not to be discouraged. From such a standpoint, one sees everything from the disappearance of the family wage, the rise of militant feminism, the mainstreaming of the sexual revolution's most radical elements, and the accelerating fall in both testosterone and sperm count, through to everyday occurrences like inordinately tight trousers, the wearing of nail varnish, and the retreat from the real realm of responsibility to the virtual one of computer games.

The growing acknowledgement of this depressing deficit in masculinity undoubtedly accounts for the international success of Jordan Peterson's *12 Rules for Life*, in which he offers some very practical and rather quotidian suggestions like "clean up your room" and "stand up straight with your shoulders back." Much of what Peterson says in these *Rules* is, of course, what every young man heard growing up until only a generation or two ago when the deception of 'personal authenticity' finally eradicated the last residue of healthy prejudice. Men thereafter began to believe the lie that self-actualisation comes by self-discovery rather than the truth that it comes by self-forgetting, and in turn they ceased to be men. Now, many men are trying to find their way back. May I, then, add my own old-fashioned 'Rule': men, start carrying pocketknives again.

# 12

# HUNTING AND
# THE MORAL LAW

ON THE FIRST PAGE OF ROGER
Scruton's *On Hunting*—his homage to foxhunting—there is a sentence which leaps
out from the page like a 17 hands Irish Hunter
risking an untrimmed blackthorn hedgerow: "Most
of those who hunt are ordinary decent people who
stand, in my experience, noticeably above the moral
norm."[1] This does not, of course, correspond well
with the popular image of people who hunt: arro-
gant toffs anxious to satiate a vulpicidal bloodlust.
Those who actually go hunting, however, have yet
to encounter such persons. Scruton's sentence is
a provocative proposition—derived from a biased
observation—but it also coheres entirely with my
own experience. On the hunting field, one routinely encounters humility, courtesy, hospitality,
and genuine inclusivity that is reminiscent of the
settled ways of an England that one discovers in
old novels, but which has since been quashed by
decades of social disruption and soft Marxism.

Perhaps it's obvious why hunting people seem
"noticeably above the moral norm." After all, their
conduct largely determines whether they will continue to be accommodated by farmers and landowners on whose lands they hunt. They are also keen
to keep their fieldsport going; hence they must
balance the sufficient exclusivity to inspire interest

---

[1] Roger Scruton, *On Hunting* (London: Yellow Jersey Press,
1999), 1.

with the necessary inclusivity to keep membership up, and given that members meet each other often throughout the Season, the rituals of communal renewal are essential to maintaining the bond—like the hunt lunches and puppy shows. Were sensitivity towards others and the habits of hospitality to wane, the hunt would dwindle.

These explanations I offer for the moral rectitude that Scruton observed in the hunting community are not, however, of adequate depth to account for it. I've been hunting with hounds on and off since I was a schoolboy and yet I feel—and probably shall always feel—like an outsider, accepted by the hunting community as a guest who can never wholly belong to it. The hunt's most revered members appear as objects of the terrain itself, whose lives and livelihood are so entangled with the cycles of the countryside that were the hunt—even in its present, impoverished form—to be legislated out of existence, so too would the very existence of these elders be snuffed out. They inhabit a world from which modernity has unhappily removed me, which I may only visit in fleeting episodes when I suspend my work as a writer to renew my covenant with the landscape on which we all ultimately depend. Thus, I enjoy the benefit of studying this community from its peripheries, and the findings of my anthropological examinations are that, when it comes to the admirable moral intuitions of hunting folk, there is something much deeper going on.

Acknowledgement of the high moral quality of people who hunt with hounds was perhaps first conveyed by William Cobbett in his *Rural Rides*. Cobbett was a keen field sportsman. He loved to shoot gamebirds, and whilst undertaking his journalistic investigations into the conditions of rustic England's working poor, he also restored himself by taking his pony to as many foxhunts as possible. Such commitment to shooting and hunting, however, permitted him to see a moral difference between the two kinds of field sportsman at play:

> There is, however, an important distinction to be made between *hunters* (including coursers) and *shooters*. The latter are, as far as relates to their exploits, a disagreeable class, compared with the former; and the reason of this is, their doings are almost wholly *their own*; while, in the case of the others, the achievements are the property of *the dogs*.[2]

Cobbett notes that people who shoot can attribute the day's successes to themselves. Someone who hunts with hounds, however, is not actually hunting at all. Rather, he is following, perhaps witnessing, at most facilitating, hunting that is carried out not by himself but by the hounds. Any successes of the day, then, are to be attributed to the quality of the pack, and not to the members of the field or the hunt staff. This, Cobbett suggests, effects very different moral characters in the two kinds of field sportsman. He continues:

> Nobody likes to hear another talk *much* in praise of his own acts, unless those acts have a manifest tendency to produce some good to the hearer; and shooters do talk *much* of their own exploits, and those exploits rather tend to *humiliate* the hearer ... whereas, hunters are mere followers of the dogs, as mere *spectators*; their praises, if any are called for, are bestowed on the greyhounds, the hounds, the fox, the hare, or the horses.[3]

---

[2] William Cobbett, *Rural Rides* (London, Penguin Books, 2001), 198.
[3] Ibid., 198-99.

For Cobbett, one ought not to speak of oneself,
unless it is thought that doing so will be of good
not to oneself but to one's converser. As a rule, for
Cobbett, you should forget about yourself and focus
on others. It is almost impossible, however, to discuss a day's shooting without referring to one's own
successes, and this, for Cobbett, introduces to the
sport a moral danger that does not exist for those
who hunt with hounds. As people boast of their
achievements in bagging braces of pheasant or partridge, their fellow field sportsmen feel compelled
to compete in the boasting of the day, and so a
culture of encouraging a moral defect is unavoidably
established. Among those who follow hounds, praise
is always reserved for the animals who pursue or
are pursued, and thus an appreciation of a world
beyond oneself is opened up, by which one can self-
forget — which is, as it happens, the first stage of
spiritual perfection.

In fact, I think that Cobbett is awfully hard on
people who shoot. Rough shooters in particular enjoy
an earthy amity, have a deep esteem for the various
birds which they look forward to eating, and share
a mysterious bond with the spaniels and retrievers
that accompany them into the undergrowth. Wild-
fowlers possess encyclopaedic knowledge of weather
patterns, tides, and migration routes of geese and
duck, and this knowledge has connected their sport
with some of the finest conservation and habitat-
preservation efforts, especially in the UK. Furthermore, a very profound love and understanding of
deer, respect for the stalking seasons that optimise
the health of the various species, and disdain for
any waste of good venison, are the absolute norm
among deer stalkers. Self-congratulatory attitudes
based on the number of 'kills' is something I simply
haven't encountered.

Nonetheless, Cobbett's observation is interesting. Indeed, the fact that there is ongoing commentary at all on the moral rectitude of those who hunt makes it worthy of some consideration, given the negative image of hunters that many moderns both accept and perpetuate—people who want to enjoy the gifts of the countryside whilst neglecting to learn anything about it.

My own view is that the relationship between hunting and highly developed moral instincts is a deep one, even if not universally observable. Traditionally-minded people have always intuited that a certain harmony exists between the natural order and the moral law. Societies that encourage—either positively or by omission—behaviour which conflicts with the moral law, soon disintegrate. And a society that undermines the natural order will find that its moral compass will corrupt. This belief in a harmony between the natural order and the moral law is one of the most elementary principles of any traditional worldview. I want to suggest that hunting with hounds arose from a moral urge to rectify a rift that had occurred in the natural order.

As the predators with which we competed for supremacy over the land declined in numbers due to our conversion of the wilderness into farmland, we discerned that a disorder had entered the natural order. Whilst we needed to farm and work the land for the sake of civilisation-building, so too species that had once been hunted by wolves and big cats had no such predators anymore. This, of course, not only caused problematic population growth (which always causes the species in question to outbreed their source of sustenance and then starve), but it also meant that sick and unhealthy members of the species were able to persist, adversely affecting the species as a whole. Looking upon this disruption

of the natural order, our ancestors set out to find
the animals that then wandered unhunted, and
they unleashed upon them a synthetic wolfpack:
hounds. By so doing, they at least partially mended
the rupture.

There were, of course, other ways to manage these
species. They could be snared, to die in agony over
several days. They could be poisoned, to die in agony
over several days. As firearms developed, they could
be shot, which could lead to wounding and a very
slow death. All these ways were both unnecessarily
harsh, uncertain, and indiscriminate, with healthy
animals being more likely killed than unhealthy
ones — the exact opposite of what is the case in
houndwork. Thus, such solutions could never have
rectified the rift in the natural order, and in some
ways would perpetuate it.

It has always puzzled me, in fact, that people
who demonise hunting with hounds remain largely
unconcerned with other kinds of wildlife management. The speed with which an animal was killed
by a pack of hounds was quite incomparable to the
often drawn-out death experience of animals once
human technology or manmade chemicals were
introduced.

We ought to be aware that the whole moral project of modernity has been one of departing from the
moral law precisely by overcoming the natural order
via ever more technology. The drama of *late* modernity is principally one of various cracks appearing after decades of our violation of the natural
order. Our hyper-mechanised agricultural industry is under-nourishing us. Our hyper-mechanised
medical industry is making us ill. Our transport
industry is making our air unclean. Our trampling
of the natural laws of family-building and procre-
ation have led to a demographic decline that will

soon see our populations terminated and replaced. By way of technology, we freed ourselves from the chains that bound us to our place in the cosmos, and, having broken those chains with the works of our hands, we have found that these manacles held us from plummeting into oblivion.

Those who hate the hunt—from my encounters with them—seem still to believe in the moral emancipation of humanity through technologization, and the sentimental illusion of 'Progress' that accompanies it. For this reason, anti-hunting sentiment has become bound up with veganism in recent years, a diet that is, in nearly all cases, more dependent than any other culinary fad on a highly technologized industry of processed foods. And that's why shotguns, rifles, and rods will never be quite so offensive to such people as a pack of hounds; a pack of hounds achieves something truly natural in a way that other fieldsports—for all their many merits—can never achieve. Hunting with hounds runs perfectly contrary to the narrative of domination over nature by use of technology, for it marks a return to the natural order and a humble submission to its ways, as well as the spontaneity that belongs to those ways. The point of controversy here, it turns out, is not that of a concern for the natural world but the will of those who would free themselves from it altogether.

I say that the drama of late modernity is one of various cracks appearing after decades of violating of the natural order, but in fact they ceased to be cracks a while ago and have become cavernous gorges. Every current unfolding political programme—whether of the new nationalisms or the new globalisms—is seeking to address the problem of how to weather the storm of modernity's final unravelling. If we've learned anything from history,

the disappearance of the ways of living to which
we're accustomed will likely coincide with mass
distrust — already emerging, in fact — among an
atomised population which possesses little to none
of the concrete and habituated knowledge on which
a responsible and accountable society can be built
up. Suddenly it will become clear that all our political squabbling was weakening us when we were
supposed to be civilisation-building, our pursuit
of personal 'authentic selfhood' was isolating us
when we were meant to be inducting ourselves into
our communities, and our construction of 'online
communities' of interfacing avatars has resulted in
no community at all.

The hunt is almost the perfect antithesis of the
'online community.' An 'online community' is a
collective established and joined by strangers who
know nothing about one another except each other's constantly ejaculated opinions. Via the 'online
community' one is re-fashioned as a bodiless, place-
less, opinion-generating spirit who can exercise the
obnoxiousness that would be impossible in person.

In the hunting community, on the other hand, we
know little of each other's opinions. We are bound
together by the landscape with which we seek ever
to intensify our intimacy. Our bond is not established by views or factions, but by our experience
of belonging and the ongoing practice of manners
that protects that experience of belonging. We have
an ancient ceremony to celebrate, a ritual in which
we momentarily mend the rupture that art brings
to nature in the perfecting of it — by which we can
also ask forgiveness from nature's Author. And we
have a job to do, a job that brings all those who
dwell in this little parcel of the world together in
a shared affirmation of the concrete community to
which we belong, and which tacitly mends the link

with our ancestors who made it all possible. As Scruton put it, reflecting on his first hunt: "Here was a piece of England which was not yet alien to itself, a community which had yet to be ground into atoms and scattered as dust."[4]

Anti-hunting activists know of each other through their shared hatred of the hunt, which they express to one another in online forums. They only meet in person when they gather with their faces covered by balaclavas to terrorise the respectable folk who manage the land—land which they proceed to trample, uninvited. They are not a community but a swarm of ghosts who incarnate themselves in passing moments of self-righteous passion, and just as quickly vanish, unaccountable to the *real* community whose shared life they have disrupted.

The hunt is certainly not the only kind of *real* community out there. There are plenty of such communities—the first in import among which is the parish—but these communities are only discovered on leaving the virtual, counterfeit community of online opinion-blurting spectres. It is necessary for those who wish to resurrect our broken world and begin anew the venture of civilisation-building to find such communities and induct themselves into their ways. By this process of organic initiation, the light of the moral law may again be rendered perceptible, which will be the first stage in mending our world.

---

4 Scruton, *On Hunting*, 45.

# 13

# SABOTEURS AND NAZISM

IT HAS NOT GONE UNNOTICED THAT the ruffians who comprise the various Antifa groups (short for 'Anti-fascists') look strikingly like fascists. They turn up at town centres or city squares to scream abuse at pro-lifers, or they physically attack supporters of some 'hate-speaker' at a university (who has likely made some shocking remark about men not being able to become women), or they assist some other aligned revolutionary group by smashing shop windows and vandalising public monuments. Members of Antifa wear black paramilitary outfits and balaclavas and are frequently found to carry batons or metal pipes. They are, in all essential things, a sort of militia of largely untraceable thugs who use verbal abuse and physical violence to terrify into silence anyone with whom they have certain ideological differences—for the purpose of establishing social uniformity. Thus, on closer inspection, it becomes clear that these people don't merely look like fascists; they *are* fascists.

The British countryside has its own paramilitary fascists. Like Antifa, they wear black paramilitary clothing and balaclavas and deploy threats and violence to frighten those with whom they disagree. They call themselves 'hunt-saboteurs' because they oppose hunting with hounds. The *way* they oppose hunting is simple: they terrorise rural communities that are trying to conserve their way of life and walk the tightrope of managing the countryside in the face of badly written regulations. In 2022, five such thugs were convicted at Loughborough

Magistrates Court for verbally abusing and punching a girl, aged 15, and two men aged 61 and 52, who had been following a trail hunt in Leicestershire. The paramilitary gang, always dressed in black with balaclavas, that was involved in this particular incident is especially notorious. Outfitted as terrorists, they have been intimidating rural communities across the North West, North Wales, and the West Midlands for years, resorting both to verbal and physical abuse at the first opportunity. In 2019, the same gang entered the property of a young couple with two children—a family who did not even have any connection with the local hunt. When the mother asked the men to remove their balaclavas and leave her property, they told her to "f**k off." As the brave mother said to their faces, these thugs are not from the countryside, they have no understanding of countryside life and rural management, and they simply want to cause trouble. In the same year, this gang's leader had already been convicted for assaulting a Huntsman.[1]

The connection between anti-hunting attitudes and fascism may, in fact, be a deep one. The prosecution of these roaming thugs reminded me of an argument developed by a philosopher friend of mine that demonstrates, as he put it, the "logical link between 'moral vegetarianism' and Nazism."

The argument begins as follows. Humans are natural omnivores. That is difficult to deny. We have the jaw structure and teeth to masticate meat, we assimilate it well, there is much nutrition that

---

[1] For a report of these stories, see Jack Elmson, "Unsettling moment terrified mother, 31, confronts masked mob of 'animal rights activists' led by convicted thug as they block drive to her rural home with Range Rover in bid to stop hunt," *Daily Mail*, October 28, 2019, https://www.dailymail.co.uk/news/article-7621355/Unsettling-moment-terrified-mother-31-confronts-masked-mob-animal-rights-activists.html.

we cannot enjoy otherwise (unless by artificially
supplementing), and we—apart from some very
rare aberrations—love the taste of it. This is not
simply a Western phenomenon. Man, instantiated
in his various cultures and communities, universally
yearns for meat.

We are naturally omnivorous. Let's agree on that.
If one chooses not to eat meat, then, it will invariably be for one of three reasons. Either one is a rare
case and simply doesn't like the taste of meat, or
one is squeamish and doesn't like the thought of
eating meat, or one deems it immoral to eat animals.
Here, we are only concerned with the third sort of
person—the 'moral vegetarian.' (There is the recent
emergence of the vegetarian or vegan who opts for
such a diet for environmental reasons but, as we
shall see, such a person is in fact covered by the
third category.) The moral vegetarian refrains from
eating meat *despite* his omnivorous nature. He thinks
that, whilst we might naturally eat meat, a moral
principle compels us to do otherwise.

But if humans ought to be vegetarian on moral
grounds, despite their omnivorous nature, then presumably all meat-eating animals should also stick to
a vegetarian diet—despite their natures. One might
reply that whilst humans can *choose* not to eat meat,
that kind of agency, as well as awareness of the
moral imperative that compels us to be vegetarian
despite our penchant for eating animals, cannot
be expected of a lion, for example. But this won't
hold. A lack of awareness of a moral imperative
may diminish—or even remove altogether—the
culpability of the agent, but those who *are* aware
of the imperative have an obligation to prevent the
agent from acting contrary to the imperative. Take,
for example, someone who is about to reverse his
vehicle over another person whom he doesn't see

because that person is crouching down; the driver may not be culpable for reversing over the person whom he cannot see, but the bystanders who witness the event are gravely culpable if they do not do all they can to prevent the driver from reversing over the crouching person whom they do see.

Lions may not be blameworthy for eating spring-bok, then, but *we* are blameworthy for not preventing lions from eating springbok and for not compelling them to adopt a vegetarian-only diet. Indeed, such a view isn't completely eccentric, given that large numbers of urban cat-owners compel their captive creatures to join them in their vegan and vegetarian diets — on moral grounds, I should add — and there are many brands on the market offering such pet foods (if, indeed, it can be called food).

If we bear such guilt, at least by omission, for not spending all our time running around the savannah trying to intervene in the hunt of the pride and steer lions away from springbok and onto some highly processed vegan gloop, by what reasoning may we absolve ourselves?

This is where the 'nature's cycle' account of meat consumption comes in. Whilst it is claimed that in a better, purer world, meat would not be consumed by any animal, the fact is that, as things stand, if predators did not eat meat then the natural culling process would come to an end. The world would then be overrun by prey animals. That, of course, would have a devastating effect on vegetation, which would then lead to the very extinction of those prey animals. Thus, whilst the moral law, as understood by moral vegetarians, would have all animals abandon the consumption of other animals, certain practical considerations require us to permit the killing of animals by animals for the sake of population control.

If, however, animals should be able to kill animals for reasons of population control despite the general moral imperative to do otherwise, then surely humans are bound by the same principle. Hence, whilst killing is wrong, and certainly killing for food is very wrong indeed, killing for the sake of population management is — in this less than perfect world — acceptable. Humans, who have no successful natural predator in the animal kingdom, are surely not exempted from this norm. Humans must, then, be subjected to various population control programmes. These programmes might even necessitate the killing of certain individuals or groups for the 'flourishing of the species.' Thus, moral vegetarianism and its more radical offspring, veganism, plausibly lead to something resembling Nazism.

This was, in any case, the argument of my friend. I choose not to name him because moral vegetarians and vegans are not known for their ability to listen dispassionately to an opposing viewpoint — the ramifications for him could be, well, *fascistic*. Whatever the merits or demerits of my friend's argument, it has certainly been somewhat inadvertently strengthened by the opinions of Peter Singer, Professor of Bioethics at Princeton University. A very vocal animal-rights campaigner and promoter of veganism, whose sentimentalism towards animals goes so far as to support bestiality, Singer has also argued at length for the moral licitness of killing of children, the disabled, and the elderly.

Now ... back to those fascists who prowl the English countryside looking for rural folk to beat up while such persons try quietly to manage the landscape for which they've cared for generations. These thugs, in fact, stand in a long and well-established tradition of Nazi vegetarians. Of course, I am fully aware that there is a popular and very lazy habit of calling your ideological opponents 'Nazis' — the *reductio ad Hitlerum* — but in this case, it's actually true. Adolf Hitler was a vegetarian explicitly on moral grounds, deeming the consumption of animals to be cruel and barbaric. The first country in the world to outlaw hunting with hounds was Nazi Germany in 1934. The Nazi regime proceeded to introduce animal welfare laws which were unparalleled at the time. The Nazi architect, Albert Speer, in his memoirs *Inside the Third Reich*, describes Hitler's recourse to vivid and gruesome descriptions of animal suffering and slaughter in attempts to dissuade his colleagues from eating meat. Chief Nazi propagandist, Josef Goebbels, wrote in his diary:

> The Führer . . . believes more than ever that meat-eating is harmful to humanity. Of course, he knows that during the war we cannot completely upset our food system. After the war, however, he intends to tackle this problem also. Maybe he is right. Certainly, the arguments that he adduces in favour of his standpoint are very compelling.[2]

Hitler was keen to promote the self-image of an animal-lover. *Neugeist/Die Weisse Fahne*, a children's Nazi magazine that was popular during Hitler's dictatorship, printed the following:

> Do you know that your Führer is a vegetarian, and that he does not eat meat because of his general attitude toward life and his love for the world of animals? Do you know that your Führer is an exemplary friend of animals, and even as a chancellor, he is not separated from the animals he has kept for years? . . . The Führer is an ardent opponent

---

[2] Joseph Goebbels, *The Goebbels Diaries*, translated by Louis P. Lochner (n.p.: Charter Books, 1993), 679.

of any torture of animals, in particular vivi-
section, and has declared to terminate those
conditions ... thus fulfilling his role as the
saviour of animals, from continuous and
nameless torments and pain.

Hitler, an early proponent of 'animals rights theory,'
a moral theory that is untenable (notwithstanding
its widespread recognition), frequently and openly
expressed his distress at stories or pictures of animal
suffering.

This may seem strange to many. How could a
man who authorised the murder of millions of people, and sanctioned the most horrendous experi-
ments on human beings, be so sensitive to animal
suffering? Well, I don't find such characteristics
contradictory at all.

It was foreseeable that moral vegetarianism would
rise in an age of counterfeit virtue, in which we're
all seeking for ways to confirm that we're really
'good people' whilst avoiding the hard work of self-
sacrifice for the sake of our neighbour. Sentimentalism directed at animals, creatures that demand no
moral growth from you and will never call you to
account, is the perfect counterfeit virtue. One can
enjoy all the feelings of righteousness and do nothing
beyond sticking to greens. Meanwhile, one is eman-
cipated from cultivating any real virtue as one's misanthropy is a part of one's counterfeit virtue. Nazism,
incidentally, is an entire system of counterfeit virtue.

Sentimentalism towards animals developed alongside modern misanthropy. As another friend of mine
put it to me, if you treat animals like humans, you
will treat humans like they're just animals; or in
Chesterton's immortal words, "Wherever there is
animal worship, there is human sacrifice."[3]

---

[3] G.K. Chesterton, *The Uses of Diversity* (n.p.: Jazzybee Verlag,
2017), 2.

# 14

# A LESSON FROM THE FESTIVAL OF HUNTING

EVERY YEAR, I ATTEND THE FES-
tival of Hunting, known in fieldsporting
circles as "the Peterborough" on account of
the town outside of which it has been held since
it was established in 1878 under the Chairmanship
of the Marquis of Huntly. The Huntsman of the
pack to which I belong is often required to judge
the beagles and harriers there.

It is a marvellous event. Examples from packs
of foxhounds, bloodhounds, fellhounds, harriers,
beagles, and bassets are all exhibited, whilst an
adrenaline-fueled inter-hunt relay takes place across
the field, from which the pounding hooves of Irish
hunter horses constantly thunders out.

I watch the judging of the packs and wander
around the kennels inspecting the specially chosen
hounds that have been brought to the show. The
Kimblewick, the Duke of Beaufort's, the Bicester
with Whaddon Chase, and many, many more foxhound packs are represented there. It is wonderful
to wander about the rings, watching the Masters of
various packs collect their rosettes with great pride.

I usually encounter enough familiar faces, and
in any case, I always have my whippet, Pico, for
companionship. There are many stalls there where
one can buy hunting coats, tweed jackets, boots,
caps, jewellery, and — much more interesting to
me — old books and glorious romantic prints in
large oak frames.

One year, I met David Thorne at the Festival, an artisan famous for his finely made hunting whips, and I asked him about a whip that I had recently acquired. I won the said beautiful, early nineteenth-century whip when attending as a friend's guest the annual hunt dinner of the Palmer-Marlborough Beagles. It was undeniably a magnificent whip, but it was in desperate need of some maintenance, as I discovered when I arrived home the day after the dinner. I had walked through the front door, and showing off what I'd won the previous night, I attempted to crack the whip—at which point it disintegrated in my hand.

I showed Mr Thorne the sorry looking bits and pieces of my hunting whip (thankfully, it was not my only hunting whip). He frowned. He didn't speak. He frowned some more. Then, he looked up and said, "That's alright. I'll deal with this. I'll have your name and address and soon get it back to you with new life in it, and with an invoice of course." We shook hands and off I went, having left him with my whip (or, rather, the various pieces of it) and my details.

I enjoy wandering between the rings where the hounds are shown, some of which no doubt have a pedigree going back to those very hounds that accompanied St Hubert at his vision of the miraculous stag. I always, however, make a point of visiting the ring where the coursing dogs—sighthounds of various breeds—are exhibited. The displaying of these cheetah-like hounds pleases me immensely. Incidentally, veteran wildlife welfare campaigner James Barrington (who also attends the Festival of Hunting) has argued that the banning of hare coursing—in no way to be compared to poaching—has been detrimental for the UK hare population. That these running dogs are still shown at the Festival, despite the fact that their role in rural management has been forbidden to them by political engineers, testifies to their importance in hunting history. Hopefully, one day, we shall see coursing dogs hunt over the landscape once more.

Coursing—the chasing of quarry by sighthounds— is in fact the oldest of all fieldsports. It was, until the reign of Queen Elizabeth I, the sport of royalty and high-ranking nobility. It was forbidden for anyone below a Duke to own a greyhound, and the slaying of a coursing dog merited punishments comparable to that for homicide. Elizabeth I was passionate about coursing and ordered the drawing up of rules, which in all essentials remained the rules under which coursing continued until 2005 when it was banned by a Labour government that had no understanding of countryside management and had no interest in learning anything about it.

One year, as I watched the handlers of grey-hounds, deerhounds, and salukis make their way to the ring, the lady who was leading them stopped and addressed me: "Excuse me," she said, "the gentleman who was meant come with a whippet was unable to make it; would you and your dog mind stepping in?" Pico, in turn, got his moment of fame as he represented his breed at the Festival of Hunting.

The Festival is an example of real culture and the celebration of an inherited and fragile way of life. That the Festival is indeed an instance of real, wholesome culture is made all the more discernible by the small group past which I and others must drive each year to get to the event. There they stand with bright blue hair, tattooed skin, contorted faces, and large signs with words such as '*Murderer!*' emblazoned upon them. From this spectacle I make my way to the Festival, where beautifully dressed,

well-mannered, orderly people greet one another and
discuss simple interests such as the mottling on this
or that foxhound or the weather of the last Season.

Comparing these two groups, I think of Roger
Scruton's meditation on the error of Rousseau:

> Conservatives . . . wish to keep the frail crust
> of civilization in place as long as possible,
> knowing that beneath it there does not lie
> the idyllic realm of Rousseau's noble savage,
> but only the violent world of the hunter-
> gatherer. Faced with civilizational decline,
> therefore, they hold . . . that "delay is life." [1]

One has the impression, on arrival at the Festival
of Hunting, of joining a people who are at home
in the world. Or, at least, they once were. That is,
they were at home in the world when the realm
that humans inhabited had been elevated out of the
"violent world of the hunter-gatherer" and transformed into a civilisation. Part of the genius of the
Western mind was that of fostering a civilisation
in such a way that didn't deny that we are, at bottom, hunter-gatherers. In turn, we recognised that
such raw hunter-gatherer material needed to be
redeemed rather than denied. We would continue
to hunt, but we'd do so in red coats in the context
of ceremony and ritual, and we would continue
to gather, but we would do it through the stable
labour of agriculture.

By this gentle transformation of the hunter-
gatherer into a bearer of human civilisation, we
found a way of remaining at home in the world
while we impressed our presence upon its face.
"Art is man's nature," Edmund Burke tells us, and
one need only to meditate on this assertion for a

---

[1] Roger Scruton, *How to be a Conservative* (London: Blooms-
bury, 2014), 165.

moment for the veracity of the claim to shine forth
so brightly that it is almost blinding. Strip away
that art in the spirit of Rousseau, and one does
not find *true human nature* underneath the surface,
but the blue-haired, tattooed banshees exploding in
frustration at their failure to make of this world a
home, rebounding that frustration onto the nicely
dressed passers-by. Rousseau was half-correct: one
will find savages, but not noble ones. Seeing nothing beyond the treacle of their own sentimentalism,
through whose sticky-sweet sludge they every day
wade in their urban cages, they don't understand
why those who daily deal in realities don't inhabit
the same world of fake emotion. Their response is
another sentiment that lies just underneath the
gushing impulses that they direct at their Disneyland conception of animals: hatred of humans.

This, I believe, reaches the heart of the matter,
and brings to the fore the great disparity between
those who hunt and support hunting on the one
hand, and those who oppose hunting on the other.
The former group, albeit in an unexamined way, see
the great imperative before us to be that of making
a home in this world, and for them that means
not flying from nature, but taking our place in the
natural world, namely as stewards over it — stewards
who have an obligation to manage it responsibly.
The latter group, quite as tacitly as the former, also
seek a home in the world, but see this to be possible
only in a flight from nature and from obedience to
its laws. They will, of course, eventually find their
home in a virtual, online world — only to discover
that it is no home at all.

Scruton used to say that there were three con-
secutive stages to his life's history: wretchedness,
uneasiness, and hunting. We must all make the
journey out of wretchedness, through uneasiness,

and onto something by which we can come to peace with the world — if only to stop ourselves from becoming a tremendous nuisance to others. The alternative is to retreat from reality and join the blue-haired banshees.

## 15

# THE THEURGY
# OF DEER STALKING

THE FIRST TIME I SHOT A DEER, it was a large fallow buck which I took down at 170 yards with a fine Finnish rifle on the fringes of a woodland in East Sussex. It was an easy shot. With my friend—a very accomplished deer stalker—I had built a hide in which we waited. As a sizeable herd emerged from the twilight shadows of the wood to graze in the meadow, my companion indicated to me which buck I ought to take. We couldn't get a clear shot with a safe backstop, so we crawled into the middle of the pasture where we lay for a few moments to control our breathing, and then, *bang*! I had intended to take a neck shot but at the last moment I lost confidence in my abilities and took a 'boiler room' shot instead, hitting it in the heart. The buck leaped into the air, took two steps, and collapsed dead. On inspecting that magnificent creature, I saw that I had hit it precisely where I had aimed, and thus could have taken my initially intended shot to the neck and spared the animal that second and a half of suffering.

Almost immediately after shooting that buck, I became aware of myself. My body had petrified with adrenaline, and my finger now stuck out straight over the trigger guard, wobbling like a twig. My muscles and bones seemed to be more aware of the gravity of the situation than any rational deliberation would have brought home. A veritable king of the woods, crowned with the champion antlers

of a rut veteran, who had for many seasons stood
with his court of hinds and ascending fawns amid
the hallowed glades of Wessex—that glorious region
where England was invented—now lay motionless
upon a muddy bed.

Unlike in continental Europe, we have no long-
standing tradition of deer stalking in England. Here,
red and fallow deer herds were historically managed
with great success by staghound and buckhound
packs, and roe deer—now called the 'prince' of British deer—were considered a mere pest and shot on
sight with shotguns until they were almost extinct
south of the border. The only great tradition of British deer stalking existed north of England, in the
Scottish Highlands, where gillies—servants who on
account of their rural knowledge have always been
respected as leaders—took wealthy sportsmen out
to stalk red stags in the hills, often combining the
use of deerhound and rifle. English deer stalking as
a fieldsport and as a means of responsible wildlife
management has a pedigree going back only to the
1950s, and it has few if any traditions attached to it.

In central Europe, following a driven hunt, it is
common for the killed animals to be arranged on
a bed of fir branches between flaming torches, and
honoured with songs and the sounding of hunting
horns. The Plains Indians of the American Midwest
danced after hunting, to honour the spirits of the
creatures that had fallen to give them sustenance,
and I am told that even in the United States of
today, many hunters kneel and praise God on making a kill. In spiritually frozen England, however,
our sporting pursuits are almost wholly without
religiosity, with some sportsmen even hunting on
Sundays. Having shot that buck, I could think of
nothing to draw upon from my own culture to
respond appropriately to the situation. A pat on

the shoulder from my fellow stalker with a "Good shot, pal!" did not correspond to the seriousness of the occasion. In truth, I was pleased both with the cleanness of the kill and the beauty of the prize, and I was looking forward to casseroling its venison, but in my wonder, I also wanted to reverence my quarry and worship its Maker.

Reverence and wonder belong to a special kind of meeting with reality. Such sentiments are similar to, but qualitatively different from, those that go by the same name but are experienced by the *observer*. The observer, whether a viewer in an art gallery or a hiker on the fells, looks out with amazement at something of which he is not a part, which he sees from the outside, so to speak, with which he has not become one thing. Those who know me know that I love both art galleries and hillwalking, but I feel sorry for people who do not know the awe that arises from deep participation. There are many ways to experience the participatory awe of which I speak (dancing being among the most important), but hunting—whether with hounds or with rifle—is particularly special to me, wherein I have experienced this awe with such intensity that it has become an addiction.

During a deer stalk, one becomes part of the landscape itself. In pursuit of prey, one crouches among the predators of the world. Even someone sympathetic to the activity may be forgiven for thinking that the use of a sophisticated technology like a rifle, with its scope and astonishing long-range accuracy, might remove one from the inner drama of the hunt. In a way, this is true. A deer stalk will never be as 'natural' as houndwork, but on the other hand, in the case of the latter, one is not hunting at all; the hounds are hunting, and the hunter is 'hunting the hounds,' and consequently

he remains more an observer of the hunt than the
actual predator. During a stalk, however, the deer
stalker *is* the hunter—he is the predator. The difference between a deer stalker with his rifle and a
hunter-gatherer with his bow and arrows is a mere
difference of degree. And deer stalkers know that
deer stalking is a deeply primal activity.

Not long after qualifying as a certified deer
stalker, I shot my first muntjac. These hardy little
creatures—not much larger than my whippet—with
their short antlers (more like little horns) and tusks,
belong to an invasive species from Asia. For their
presence in England, we can thank the Bedfords—
that most whiggish of families that gave us the
philosopher Bertrand Russell (who thankfully was
humbled by the inestimable Wittgenstein)—from
whose Woburn Abbey muntjacs escaped sometime
in the late nineteenth century. I lay prone upon a
hill and the animal wandered out into the open
below. I put my crosshairs on it and the kill was
instant. Later that week, I cooked the haunches in
red wine, beef stock, thyme, and juniper berries,
and with roast potatoes and Yorkshire puddings
I ate them with my children, while my vegetarian
wife looked on quizzically.

Muntjac have no close season, and so they can be
stalked alongside roe bucks in midsummer. There
is nothing like a summer stalk. To move along the
skirt of a wood, silently prowling as the sun sets
and blushes the heavens in an apricot marvel, to
peer past a line of swaying silver birches—those
arboreal ghosts—to the maze of ancient beeches and
oaks, catching a random glimpse of movement and
freezing in anticipation, alert to every snort and
rustle, is an experience that cannot be compared to
anything else. The union of moral gravity, aesthetic
spectacle, and embeddedness in the most real level

of reality leaves one feeling more alive than I can convey, and all in the face of death.

Not discounting my defence of the primal realism of hunting with a firearm, the presence of such a sophisticated piece of technology as a modern rifle ought to give us pause for thought. Each technological step we have taken as a civilisation has undoubtedly made our lives more bearable, but so too each step has removed us from reality and moved us towards virtual substitutes. The moment man ceased to break his nails by tilling the earth with his fingers and opted for a stick, he took a step away from starvation as a constant danger over his life. But so too, at that moment the earth below his feet became 'soil,' a mass of dark matter rather than the fermenting medley of dirts, grits, twigs, bugs, seeds, stones, slimes, and everything else that makes up the fundamental prerequisite on which our agronomy depends. The technology was introduced, the reality was distanced, and with that the living earth became 'stuff.'

With each new technology, the particular becomes less particularised and more abstract, and at each technological step the abstractionist, mechanistic metaphor steps further to the fore as the dominant prism through which we see everything. Thus, with each step, our survival indeed becomes more of a given, but so too our survival is enjoyed in a greyer, more abstract world that increasingly exists in our minds alone. With each step, we increasingly retreat from anything to do with the actual complexus with which we're surrounded and of which we're a part, and we enter a world of our own making—which is really a fantasy. Our civilisation, as it became more civilised, in contending with this problem of losing grip on reality in our pursuit of safety, placed hunting at the heart of its shared culture. Our civilisation did this so that it had a lifeline.

There are, of course, *pragmatic* justifications for deer
stalking. At present, there are more deer in the UK
than at any time since the end of the Ice Age. Over
1.5 million deer roam these isles in six species, only
two of which are indigenous; and with no natural
predators besides humans, they are doing untold
damage to woodlands and our agriculture. Some
years ago, out on a hike, my son and I observed
that half a barley field had been flattened by the
Chinese water deer that have come to dominate the
Home Counties and East Anglia since they escaped
from Whipsnade Zoo in the early twentieth century.

Rewilders, wanting to leave nature to flourish
unmanaged, have recurrently run up against the
cervine problem, and found themselves — perhaps
contrary to their principles — calling on stalkers
to prevent the consumption of every newly planted
sapling. Deer devastate woodland beds, eating the
wildflowers, many of which are already in decline. In
Scotland, the country's red deer population has dou-
bled in the last fifty years, stripping the Highlands
of its already thin vegetation, sometimes in herds
of a thousand strong. And the British Deer Society
claims that deer may be responsible for a recorded
50 percent reduction in our woodland bird species,
including the blackcap, nightingale, and willow tit.

The obvious tension between a growing deer population and certain objectives of environmentalists
has meant that individual deer stalkers as well as
the estates that offer stalking packages to sporting
tourists are not targeted in the same way as the
traditional hunts and — more recently — the com-
mercial shoots. In fact, the environmentalist lobby
routinely calls for a 50-60 percent reduction in the
country's deer population. Stalkers, on the other
hand, have in general asked for a more moderate
approach to deer management, encouraging greater

interest in their sport and promoting venison as a healthy, sustainable, and organic source of protein. But given that do-gooders from the growing towns attack both the hunts and the shoots with clear ignorance of the compelling animal welfare and wildlife management arguments in their favour, it likely won't be long before deer stalkers face the same forces of 'progress' as well.

Notwithstanding the problems deer cause, only some of which I have noted, it would be a mistake to point the finger at deer for all our conservation problems — *that* would be both untrue and unjust. The roads and motorways, the heavy traffic, the UK's human population boom, the ongoing urban sprawl, the use of pesticides and herbicides, and many other factors are contributing to the erasure of the wild world of which we are meant to be responsible stewards. Nonetheless, if we're going to take our stewardship seriously, part of that will be managing our deer properly. In any case, besides having an adverse effect on biodiversity, overpopulation can lead to food shortages for the deer themselves, and consequently malnourishment and disease among them.

The many pragmatic reasons for deer stalking, however, do not sufficiently explain our need not only to continue the sport but to encourage others to take it up recreationally. The deeper reason we must stalk deer is to maintain our humanity, as the forces of modernity seek to undermine it.

The foxhunter, the beagler, the rough shooter, the fly fisher, the deer stalker: each throws himself back into reality to a depth that is perhaps impossible otherwise. A chicken wrapped in plastic, taken off the shelf from a long line of identical objects isn't *a* chicken at all, but is merely chicken. That is to say, the particularity of *this* animal which lived in

misery and died so that half of it could be binned
and the rest consumed in front of a TV, is lost on
everyone involved in its life and death. But the
muntjac I shot earlier this year, the moment I put
my crosshairs on it, ceased to be a mere instance
of its species-kind and became *this* particular wild
animal, now enjoying its habitat in peace and soon
to be offered in a disposition of admixed ecstasy and
sorrow, as a solemn sacrifice to the cosmic cycle of
death and regeneration.

Turning against hunting, perhaps our last cultural lifeline to reality, and condemning it in a
frenzy of sentimental hatred, has coincided with
our final retreat into a virtual world. We increasingly live second lives as computerised avatars in
an unreal realm of mechanised mirages, glued to
devices through dopamine dependencies. This trajectory marks a last Manichean effort to liberate
ourselves from our bodies as we are re-created in
a new bodiless Metaverse.

There is a manic hatred of the body that runs
through all modernity's new pathologies: skin pig-
ment as the source of all social ills, bodily sex-
uality as that from which we must be liberated,
masculinity as the foundation of cultural toxicity.
This hatred of the incarnational belongs to a kind
of misanthropy that is alien to the field sportsman. For him, reality must be honoured and not
repudiated, and death must be both redeemed and
judged a means of redemption. The alternative is
to seethe before reality and one's place in it, hating
the absence of the eternal in a finite universe and
hysterically endeavouring to create eternity *ex nihilo*
in a simulated world.

Having undergone a dramatic departure from the
real to the abstract through technological transformation, we are deeply disturbed by the concrete and

the actual. The obvious indication of this discomfort with reality is displayed by the confused and fiery emotions that fieldsports provoke in much of the public. But having personally sought deep encounters with *the real* for years by way of therapeutic outings with hound and gun, I am *still* struck dumb in the face of reality.

Some years back, while walking in a vale with my dog, I met a man sitting at a small wooden table, on which were about a hundred jars of honey, divided up into dark and light honeys. "Are you the beekeeper?" I asked. "I am," replied the man. "And where do you keep the bees?" "In the next field," he responded as he pointed to a collection of hives beyond a nearby fence. "Why are some jars dark," I enquired, "and some light in colour?" "Some of the colonies favour those bushes over there, and some those over there," he said, waving his hand around, "they are different plants and so with them the bees produce different honey."

I stared at that man in amazement. Everything involved in the production of this honey was before me: the beekeeper, the bees and their hives, the bushes that the bees had harvested, even the small wooden table that the beekeeper had carried from his kitchen and converted into a shop. It was all before me in a single vision and the luminous concreteness of it was dazzling. I bought eight jars of honey from that man and carried them back in my rucksack.

As it happens, the UK is the world's biggest importer of Chinese honey. Enter any supermarket in the UK and look at their own-brand honey, a jar of which can be bought for seventy pence, and you will see that it says "100% pure," with nothing to indicate the country of origin. It is, of course, from China; and routine laboratory testing reveals that much of the global supply is diluted with corn syrup. We cannot

be shocked by this, because the fact is, we're all impli-
cated in this nonsense. We all know that a jar of 100%
pure honey cannot be exported around the world
and sold for seventy pence — profit would be impossible. So, we silence the pangs of our consciences: we
require the jar's label to say 'organic' — whatever that
means in this context — and have on it a stylised
picture of a beehive in a field. We don't mind being
lied to, for by so being, *we* can claim to be the innocent party and never fess up to the fact that we're all
willingly peddling the lie together.

Our honey consumption is just one of a million
possible examples that illustrate modern man's preference for illusion over reality, and the way this
habituated preference conditions his whole life. We
are all incriminated in the self-destructive flight
from reality. Over time, we discovered that unreality
was *easier* than reality, and we agreed to be part of
the lie if the dividends were desirable enough. And
as we plunged ourselves into the web of deceptions
that became our technologized modernity, we grew
evermore troubled by our intermittent encounters
with the concrete and the actual. This is why, as
modernity continues to escalate, the field sportsman —
who is largely defined by his having made peace with
reality — will be looked upon with increasing horror.
Perhaps nothing exemplifies this better than the progressive who expresses his disdain for hunting whilst
enjoying a deep-fried battery chicken.

There is currently so much talk of 're-enchanting'
our world because people intuit that the world is
*actually* enchanted, but due to our flight from reality
we just cannot see that it is enchanted anymore. A
magical world is not a creation of folk-imagination,
but folk-imagination is generated by encounters with
the magical world — which is the way the world *is*
when known at the deepest depths of reality. One

catches a glimpse of it when one is fully absorbed in a task that quietens the mind and allows one to focus on the *actual*. In that state of near total self-forgetfulness, the world ceases to be 'stuff' and becomes a living being and a being animated by incalculable life. This intense immersion in the real is not dissimilar to what the psychologist Mihály Csíkszentmihályi called the "flow state." And as the brilliant philosopher and cognitive scientist John Vervaeke has pointed out, accumulating data suggests that depression is profoundly linked to the deficit of 'flow' in modern life.

Unfortunately, as Vervaeke has also noted, we have created counterfeit flow states through video games, which stimulate in the participant all the hyperfocus without any of the embodiment, effecting not reverence and wonder but the 'gamer rage' phenomenon on which there is mounting commentary among psychologists. Rather than feeling cleansed and awoken by the concentrated attentiveness provoked by genuine 'flow,' gamers routinely feel jaded and irritated after playing, with many feeling that they've wasted valuable time. As a friend of mine said about his son, "Every time he finished playing his video games, he was pissed off with everyone, and neither we nor he knew why." This describes a completely different effect to that experienced by the martial artist, the rock-climber, or the field sportsman—that is, by someone who has experienced real 'flow.'

In antiquity, among the Platonic schools of the Mediterranean, ecstatic immersion in the flow state was sought through theurgical practices. In theurgy, supplicatory rituals were executed to uncover the hidden presence of the gods, ultimately for the practitioners to achieve *henosis*—that is, union with the spirits. Through rites, dancing, chanting, the burning of incense, and the igniting of fires, all in a great sacral theatre deep underground in the belly of the earth, philosophers of old would peer through the veil of epistemic illusion and gaze upon uncovered realities. Together, they would pursue a full encounter with the magical realm that exists at the heart of all being.

Following their secret theurgy in hallowed caves, those mystic philosophers would practise incubation, entering a deep sleep so as to awaken the next morning *changed*. Incubation was also practised by Christians at their shrines and altars during the early centuries of the Church. This should not surprise us, but perhaps it does, for what most of us do not realise is that *theurgy baptised* is what Christian liturgy is. Christian liturgy is meant to cast the baptised community into ultimate reality, as God is called down into the inner chamber for the exoteric transformation of the world and the esoteric transformation of the soul. We, however, have grown blind to the true vitality of liturgy, and our current liturgical practices exemplify our spiritual sightlessness.

I wonder whether this spiritual blindness stems from our losing the sense of the immanence of the sacred. Part of the problem no doubt derives from the widespread insistence that Christianity is a purely monotheistic religion. Of course, in a univocal sense this is correct. But the notion that we cannot speak of Christianity as polytheistic in an analogical, but nonetheless true, sense is due to the mistaken belief that the difference between monotheism and polytheism is that of believing in one God or many. In fact, the difference between monotheism and polytheism is that of whether the divine is utterly transcendent or immanent.

The Norse gods, for example, were not gods in the sense of creators whose essence was their existence (of which there could not logically be more than one in any case). These gods were themselves created, according to Snorri Sturluson's thirteenth-century *Poetic Edda*, which explains that from the original abyss came forth a fire that melted an ice sheet, with the drops forming themselves into giants as well as a huge cow, the latter of which licked into being the first tribe of gods from a salty rock.

The origin story of the Norse gods isn't dissimilar to that of the Greek gods. In Greek mythology, in the beginning there was Chaos. Out of the chaotic void emerged the Earth and the underworld. From the sky came the Titans. Cronus, one of the Titans, castrated his father and threw the testicles into the sea, an act which produced the first of the gods, Aphrodite. Because Cronus had betrayed his father, he feared that his offspring would do the same to him. Each time his sister-wife Rhea gave birth, Cronus ate the child (famously depicted by Goya in the 1820s). But Rhea hid one child, Zeus, wrapping a stone in the baby's blanket so that Cronus ate the stone instead. When Zeus was grown up, he drugged his father, causing him to vomit up Rhea's other children (and the stone), after which Zeus fought Cronus for the kingship of the gods. Zeus and his siblings—the Olympians—were victorious, and all the Titans were hurled down into the Abyss.

The gods of old, then, were not creators but were themselves created. They were bound up with the world, their destiny being inseparable from that of the world, and they were constantly involved in the drama of the world. Anyone who has lost himself in the epics of Homer will know how entangled in that drama the gods really were. In the Christian account, the Creator is not *a* being, but is *Being*. The Creator is utterly transcendent, *He who is that is*, the infinite divine Substance of Love united in a consubstantial Triune Godhead. And yet, He is

emanated in the world not only in the creation
we see about us but in the saints and angels who
participate in His divine attributes, especially His
omnipresence and omnipotence, to which He grants
them a share. These spiritual persons are intimately
involved in the world's events, and they are as different from one another as water is from fire, down
to every angel possessing his own distinct nature.

Thus, whilst Christians believe in the God who
is Being itself and who is the Absolute Source of all
contingent beings, without whom nothing can be
explained — that is, an utterly transcendent God —
Christians also believe in *the gods*: divinised, deified
beings whose lives are bound up with our lives here
below. Foreshadowing this belief, the second-century
Platonist, Maximus of Tyre, wrote the following:

> There is one God, the king and father of all
> things, and many gods, sons of God, ruling
> together with Him. This the Greek says, and
> the Barbarian says, the inhabitant of the
> continent, and he who dwells near the sea,
> the wise and the unwise. And if you proceed
> as far as to the utmost shores of the ocean,
> there also there are gods, rising very near
> to some, and setting very near to others.[1]

According to Maximus of Tyre, all peoples know
that there is one God and that this world is full
of His gods, who in His service govern the cosmos
with Him. And given that the Christian religion
redeems this basic understanding common to all
peoples, thereby illumining the universal, primitive
theology — the "prisca theologia" as Marsilio Ficino
termed it — with the story of salvation, there follows

---

[1]  Quoted in Thomas Taylor's Introduction to Iamblichus, *On
the Mysteries of the Egyptians, Chaldeans, and Assyrians* (n.p.: Adan-
sonia Press, n.d.), xi.

an imperative for the baptised to meet these gods and know them by name. It is as "the God of gods," as the Book of Deuteronomy puts it (Deuteronomy 10:17), that the baptised must encounter the Creator; only then can they "give thanks to the God of gods, for His steadfast love endures for ever" (Psalm 136:2).

Moreover, among the gods there is one to whom Christians should give themselves in devotion before all others. Every ancient religion has an 'Earth Mother' or 'Great Mother,' who is the virginal embodiment of the whole created order, which is itself feminine as the Creator is masculine. With the discipling of the nations, the Earth Mother was revealed to be Mary, the mother of Jesus Christ. In the Christian account, she is that part of creation which is redeemed before the redemption. She is the one from whom the Eternal Son draws His sacred humanity, uniting Deity and creation in one person. Thus, she is the perfect emanation of divinity within the created order. She contains the whole of creation in her acceptance of the Incarnation, as the portal through which the Divine Logos bursts into the world that He has made. She is, therefore, intimately bound up with the earth and its story. That is why her cult utilises so many symbols of nature — roses, lilies, daffodils, irises, marigolds, cornflowers, wheat, almonds, strawberries, pomegranates, pears — and she is honoured with titles like 'Our Lady of the Fields.'

Those who hold to apostolic Christianity do not like to admit that Mary is 'worshipped' because they are on their guard against the charges of idolatry that will be hurled by protestants, but by this evasion they dishonour her. *Hyperdulia* is the worship offered to Mary alone — whom all Christians were content to call the 'Divine Mother' until the sixteenth century — for while she certainly cannot receive the *latria* of the Holy Trinity, she is

incalculably above the *dulia* of the lesser gods. And
when Christians worship the Magna Mater, they
routinely do so at grottos, where she is met enfolded
in the earth: it is with the earth's story that she is
forever bound up as 'Queen of the Universe,' with
the moon as her footstool and a constellation for
a crown (Apocalypse 12:1).

Christianity, then, ultimately reconciles monotheism and polytheism by affirming the utter unicity
and transcendence of God whilst simultaneously
seeing the world as pregnant with divinised beings
whose everlasting lives are interwoven with the
cosmic drama into which we've been thrown. Truly,
the Christian God is "the God of gods." And God
threw Himself into that cosmic drama so that He,
as Aquinas put it, "might make men gods."[2] (Once
we see this, we can grasp how far a modern Christian liturgy—commonly a trite mutual-affirmation
session—has departed from the theurgic immersion
in the spiritual realities that it is supposed to be.)

The woodland gods—Hubert, Eustace, Cóemgen,
Neot, Hildegard, Francis—all accompany me into
the wild. The great hunter-kings of old, who continue their reign at Europe's high altars—Edward
of England, Louis of France, Stephen of Hungary—
ride out before me, flushing the game from hidden
sanctuaries. I venture forth, begging permission of
the innumerable, potent spirits who guard the paths,
the groves, and the glades, whom we can no longer
see and thus whose entitlements we disregard. The
trees breathe, and I breathe their breath; the earth
pulses with the movement of the gods; a thousand
animal voices declare that the Lord is present, and
I am in Him.

In the thrill of a deer stalk, the world around
ceases to be 'stuff out there' and is revealed to be

---

[2] Thomas Aquinas, *Opusc.* 57:1-4.

what it really is, a divine communication that truly conveys the Creator as my speech truly conveys me. The magical language of God, spoken in billions of beings both visible and invisible, is whispered into my ears. His purposes are orchestrated all around via His gods. The Earth Mother, Our Lady of the Fields, blesses me and blesses my rifle. She also blesses the deer on which my offspring and I will feed, having offered its flesh in our thanksgiving to the one Lord and Creator in whom "we live and move and have our being," as the Apostle said in Athens, when he quoted a theurgic master (Acts 17:28).

In stalking deer, I peer through the web of technological layers by which we've covered up the cosmic commotion and all its grit. I become a predator who is contiguous with the whole drama of creation, pursuing prey and seeking to honour it in the kill. I find myself once more in the soul-shaking cycle of death and regeneration which never in fact disappeared, but which we hid in battery-cages and sanitarily repackaged in cellophane. Late modernity's grey oppression is seen for what it is, a thin and fragile sheet of ephemeral mist. The colourfulness of God's created language, His animating spirit unfolding in all the marvellous bits and pieces that make up our earthly home, comes bounding into my purview and strikes me dumb. And in stalking a hart and wondering at its majesty amid my act of violence, I find that I must give up nothing of my humanity but rather I must become fully human.

Anyone who has squeezed a trigger and watched the most noble of creatures collapse into a lump of lifeless matter, well knows that peculiar admixture of joy and compunction that only makes sense when accompanied by wonder. After I shot my first fallow buck, my stalking companion shot two more deer in its herd. We exhausted ourselves dragging them up the hill. Then the gralloching began at our shelter while the third member of our party, who had stayed back at the camp, threw together a welcome meal of beefsteaks and rice on a portable gas stove. We sat to satiate our appetites. There was fresh blood on our boots, on our trousers, on our hands. Under a silvery blanket of stars, accompanied only by the melody of hooting owls and rustling leaves, and beside our motionless quarry, we opened a bottle of good red wine. Enwrapped by the becharmed aroma of fried beef, the claret's bouquet, and the lingering tang of cervine bile, perennial meaning revealed itself in the concreteness of the actual, and it was glorious.

In the modern world, there are so few ways by which we can face deep reality through participatory wonder, and there are so many ways by which we're offered counterfeit versions that only exacerbate our frustration. Fieldsports thus offer a haven. The deer stalker moves in the magical atmosphere that is found in the most profound encounter with the real, in an enchanted territory which all our ancestors knew before we undertook our retreat from reality. The moral character of the deer stalker — his longing for a clean kill and his admiration for his victim — is inseparably bound up, whether he knows it or not, with this deep encounter with reality. Such a moral relation with a chased animal belongs to an ethical realm that is unknown to someone who only meets dead animals on supermarket shelves.

Fieldsports are under attack, in the UK and in many other countries. We are told by the engineers of our brave new world that soon we will all reside in '15-minute cities,' 'net-zero' urban cages from which we will never stray beyond a street or two. We will all be vegan, and we will visit our loved ones via Zoom. Our parting with reality will be complete, and we will have become what we previously ate: we will be battery animals. This process of unwinding reality—or seeking to do so through a mounting promethean pathology—we are told is necessary to save the planet from a 'climate-apocalypse,' when in fact we don't even know what the planet is anymore.

I suspect that the reasons we're offered by trans-national elites and their acolytes for this forced global transition to a 'net-zero' world are not the *real* reasons, which likely have a lot more to do with the coalescing of power. Obviously, we must slam the brakes on the technologically driven corruption of our world and its fragile climates and complex ecosystems, but the people suited to lead the charge are not the rapacious globalists in their private jets. And, since each time one of those elites starts talking about 'environmentalism,' our inbuilt bullshit-detectors start beeping, there is likely something else altogether at play.

The fact is, we declared that God is dead, and now we cannot bear it when He speaks. He speaks in His creation; and so, we are making a creation of our own where He isn't permitted to reside and where we will not be tormented by His voice. Of course, like the Tower of Babel, the whole thing will collapse. In the meantime, however, we must resist. We must resist by leaving the Tower and going deep underground, into the secret caves and sacred glades where reality is protected by the Great Mother's command, and there we must keep the theurgy of the woodlands going.

# THE PHILOSOPHY OF TOXOPHILY

## I: ARCHERY AS CIVILISATION

My friend and I stood in a large fenced-off garden at the back of his farmstead, looking down the lawn at a 3D target, a big foam boar propped up by an iron peg at the far end. An arrow was 'nocked' onto my friend's hand-woven Flemish twist string. He drew it back to his cheek bone where it remained for half a second before the elven limbs of his finely made field-recurve bow sprang forward, 'loosing' the arrow, whose brass-finished head a millisecond later sunk deep into the false creature's chest. "Shot!" I exclaimed, at which he nodded, carefully masking his self-satisfaction but not wholly succeeding in doing so. His teenage son stood by with a tray on which sat two china cups filled with strong tea. We sipped our tea and made appreciative noises towards the boy. And turning back to our counterfeit quarry, I placed an arrow that I had made some years ago (and had served me very well) onto the string of my longbow. The shaft stood to attention next to the arrow that it had followed.

Shooting those arrows made for a blissful afternoon, and a fitting way to prepare for a lecture on the anthropological assumptions of moral progressivism which I delivered an hour later to a room full of gentlemen who, from what I could tell, wholly belonged in spirit to a nobler era than the one in which we've been caught stumbling about in the dark. It was for this reason, perhaps, that

archery was an apt preparation, for those hours of
toxophilite leisure had something of the eighteenth
century about them.

I took up archery in my early teenagerhood, and
I did so—with its link to the ancient world and its
slowly learned cryptic terminology—essentially for
reasons of nostalgia. Nostalgia is typically considered today only in pejorative terms, but really the
word denotes a deep and noble brace of emotions,
perhaps the most upright emotions we shall ever
possess. *Nostalgia* is a strange Latinised Greek compound consisting of the Homeric word *nóstos*, meaning 'homecoming,' and *álgos*, meaning 'sorrow.' This
concoction of ancient Hellenic idioms and Latin
rule-bending was coined at the beginning of the
eighteenth century and encapsulates the story of
that era in the larger drama of the West.

Englishmen, looking over the Channel and seeing
the disappearance of old Europe and the arrival
of *the Enlightenment*—a euphemism for intellectual,
moral, and political darkness—were filled with
nostalgia. In obedience to this composite of emotions, and in protest against the looming modern
world, they took up the longbow (a weapon that
had laid dormant since the Tudor-era humanist
Roger Ascham made a last defence of it with his
1545 book *Toxophilus*, which was also the first defence
of it in the English language).

Many archery clubs were founded in the eighteenth century, expressing a neo-medievalism that
celebrated Merry England, complete with elaborate
knightly costumes and all the pageantry of a Renaissance festival. Membership to such clubs was exclu-
sive to the aristocracy, excluding the rising middle-
class Whigs who had captured England at the
ousting of the Stuarts. Those whiggish conspirators
might have grabbed everything else, it was thought,

but they weren't going to claim the *old* England that they'd vanquished. (Incidentally, one of the oldest of these clubs, The Royal Company of Archers, which functions as the sovereign's bodyguard north of the border, was very much on show during the UK's mourning for Queen Elizabeth II.)

The landed classes looked back to the pre-modern age, to Robin Hood and the archers of Agincourt, and significantly they took up the weapon of the peasantry, emphasising the class-fraternity of our feudal past. The bow was important as a weapon in this regard because it safeguarded chivalric duty. In pre-modern warfare, war was devastating not to the peasantry, but to the nobility. The role of the peasantry was to stand on a hill and shoot arrows for the first hour of the battle and then retreat to safety. On the field itself, it was chiefly armoured nobles that were to be found. The worst a peasant might reasonably expect was the death of their lord and his replacement with another, leaving their own lives largely unchanged since feudal laws prohibited pushing them off the land. By the bow, the peasantry could unite themselves to the cause of their feudal lord without losing their privileges as non-combatants. Not so in modern war, where the political classes sit in boardrooms while the common man is sent towards oncoming bullets.

Many eighteenth-century Englishmen sensed that for all the talk of progress, equality, freedom, and so forth, something nasty, cold, and unthinking had possessed Europe—an intuition that, like a great lamp uncovered, would soon shine forth in the blindingly clear oratory of Edmund Burke. The reasonable, trustworthy, just, and decent emotional response to this rebellion by one age against all antecedent ages was that of a deep-felt nostalgia, expressed in spasms of eccentricity, foremost among

which was the choice of the nobility to practice the
art of the longbow.

Interestingly, archery boomed in cultural importance among this class at the same time as that
other curious English habit, foxhunting. Both
forms of leisure seemed to capture the beauty of
the pre-modern agrarian life that was so rapidly
vanishing. What is especially striking is that these
two sports, whilst governed by norms regarding
the social statuses of their practitioners, were open
equally to both sexes. Women, in fact, almost immediately dominated the archery range as they did the
hunting field. (As it happens, there are two sports
that seem to best magnify the elegance that is the
peculiar possession of the fairer sex, those being
equestrianism and archery—that observations of
this kind are unfashionable make them no less
true.) As the spectre of modernity spread its grey
presence across old Christendom, of which women
no less than men are the victims, those forgotten
pleasures of our forebears—the art of the bow and
the chase—became havens for those whose remaining boast was their descent from stock who rode
chargers into battle so that bowmen could return
to their homesteads.

For these eighteenth-century reactionary aristocrats, there was something mysterious about running one's fingers down the painted feather fletching
of an arrow as it was nocked onto the bowstring,
drawing back the shaft to one's 'anchor,' looking
out at the 'boss,' and that moment—eternal and
yet fleeting—of complete mental silence before the
arrow soared from the corner of one's mouth at
two hundred feet per second, appearing with perfect imminence on the target. *I* know that something mysterious was deeply felt in the repetition
of these shots by eighteenth-century romantics as

they united themselves to the arrow in the hope that it would carry them back to Merry England, because I too have felt it.

When one stands with a longbow in hand, a quiver full of arrows on one's back, stroking the taut string with fingers encased in a leather shooting glove, it is simply impossible to resist the storming duo of emotions that together are named *nostalgia*. At that moment, one knows in the veiled recesses of one's heart that an ancient ceremony is about to be performed that has pleased the gods since time immemorial, for which they have kept the enemy out and food coming in.

Occasionally, I disappear to perform this ritual in secret. I put my bow and quiver in the car and drive out to some unvisited part of the surrounding countryside. I place my portable archery target in a field, and for an hour I shoot it at various distances. (Lawyers dispute whether Englishmen are still legally required to undertake two hours of longbow practice per week, hence it is quite possible that in these excursions I may merely be fulfilling a civic obligation.) Standing there, surrounded by the rolling arable hills of everlasting England, for a moment I incarnate the centuries. Suddenly, this world, inhabited by so many objects that appear to come from another planet and have no place here — from the automobile to the iPhone, all of which have cruelly colonised my otherwise happy life — is a world that nonetheless becomes a home again. This mystical moment is always admixed with deep sadness, reflecting that this world has become a home only in a passing instant by my performing of a ceremony that suspends me above my epoch, and at its closing rite — with the unstringing of the bow — will send me crashing back to the technologized nightmare into which we've all sleepwalked.

These two aspects of the nostalgia felt in the toxophilite ritual, the homecoming and the sorrow of
the bowman, are impeccably expressed respectively
in the paintings—both named *The Archers*—by Sir
Joshua Reynolds and Sir Henry Raeburn. Reynolds' painting (opposite, above) depicts two high
tory aristocrats, one with an Ottoman-style horse
bow and the other with a classic English longbow,
illustrating that between Albion and Anatolia lay
a whole civilisation—namely Christendom—conserving our link with which was the old tory cause
(something those who adopt the name of 'tory' today
have entirely forgotten). With all the colour and
vibrance of a medieval cathedral, the noble figures
reel and leap as they lose themselves in the hunt
amid a sacred glade. Here, in a final English attempt
at baroque excitement, *nature* and *civilisation*—contra
Rousseau—appear as two aspects of a single reality,
the latter being the former realised in human form.

Raeburn's painting (opposite, below), on the other
hand, presents all the sorrow of a kingdom that
has ceased to be a home. Two Scottish Whigs linger together in a great blanket of beige, since any
more colour would undermine the supreme puritan
virtue of moderation that replaced the *agape* of true
religion in these isles. These figures lurk, ghost-
like, as if trapped in the frame somewhere between
the realm of the living and the spiritual Hades
of modernity, the earthly realisation of the latter
being their whiggish mission. Raeburn's painting
conveys all the misery of a lost home, and in so
doing anamnestically presents the dominant emotion
felt in the soul of the modern archer.

Nostalgia is the most natural set of emotions, and
it is precisely because we are waging a war on human
nature that we struggle to use the term in any way
but negatively. And because nostalgia is so natural to

Sir Joshua Reynolds, *The Archers*, 1769

Henry Raeburn, *The Archers*, ca. 1790

us, it will always be linked to archery, the practice of
which is as natural to humans as its accompanying
feelings. In fact, if I were to stray into Jungian territory, I would say that archery is *archetypal*. Whether
in the *eros* released by Cupid's love-arrows, or the
nourishment enjoyed by the shooting of Diana's
bow, or the ultimate act of self-gift in martyrdom
by the arrows planted in St Sebastian's muscles,
archery reflects our most intense aspirations and
needs down the centuries. Just as personal growth
coincides with the exposure of our weaknesses, so
our civilisation unfolded from the meeting of Paris's
arrow with Achilles' heel. And if any further proof
were needed that archery is inextricably bound up
with perennial nostalgia, consider the supreme story
of homecoming and sorrow, namely that of Odysseus,
who reclaimed his ancestral lands by bathing them
in blood spilled by his arrows.

Practiced by every civilisation as well as every
primitive people, from the moment we could put a
stick and string together we did so to conquer our
enemies, protect our spouses, and feed our children —
and every people in the world did the same thing.
When one picks up a traditional bow (whether a
longbow, horse bow, field-recurve, or some other
type) it is as if a hidden kernel of innate knowledge,
mysteriously drawn from the totality of human
experience — a *gnosis* that has both anticipated and
directed one's life — is freed and takes possession
of oneself. The bow, we might say, is a channel by
which to receive the spirit of our ancestors.

People like me see their whole lives as a continuous struggle to claim what belonged to their ancestors, everything that modernity has declared is not
worth the trouble, which alone suffices to convince
us that modernity is rooted in a lie. Archery, however, takes that great inheritance of which we've been

robbed and retrieves it in distilled and concentrated form. And if we do not rescue our civilisational inheritance through archery, we must do so by some other means that inducts us into that civilisation in an *embodied way*, for he who fails to incarnate his inheritance in his very person never knows himself. For this reason, archery, an art that is both so universal and yet so particular, emerging everywhere on earth and yet remaining as diverse as the earth's peoples, having lost its status as a skill that was necessary for survival, has continued as a discipline of self-knowledge, self-mastery, and ultimately self-giving—what the ancients called *kenosis*. It is this aspect of archery, namely its role as a pathway to interior liberty, to which I shall now turn.

## II: ARCHERY AS SELF-MASTERY

Nearly two decades have passed since the day I stumbled upon a text to which I have returned many times since. Browsing my father's library, I spotted the slim volume: *Zen in the Art of Archery* by Eugen Herrigel. As I flicked through the opening pages, my eyes fell upon the following words:

> Should one ask ... how the Japanese Masters understand this contest of the archer with himself, and how they describe it, their answer would sound enigmatic in the extreme. For them the contest consists in the archer aiming at himself—and yet not at himself, in hitting himself—and yet not himself, and thus becoming simultaneously the aimer and the aim, the hitter and the hit. Or, to use some expressions which are nearest the heart of the Masters, it is necessary for the archer to become, in spite of himself, an unmoved centre. Then comes the supreme and ultimate miracle: art becomes 'artless,'

> shooting becomes not-shooting, a shooting
> without bow and arrow; the teacher becomes
> a pupil again, the Master a beginner, the end
> a beginning, and the beginning perfection.[1]

These sentences enthralled me. I drew the book from
the shelf and read it in a single sitting, and on
closing it I vowed to practice the art of archery.
Archery, this small book taught me, was not — as
I had thought it to be — a mere quirky hobby practiced by people who like the outdoors, but poten-
tially something much more: a path to self-mastery.

The archer, according to Herrigel, is not in fact
concerned with hitting the target, which he does
only as the external expression of the interior struggle he is undertaking. Herrigel insists that the archer
is seeking to hit *himself*, and he only truly becomes
an archer when the self has been pierced by his own
spiritual arrows. But here is the *true* archer's paradox:
to seek to hit the self is to be preoccupied with the
self, and therefore always to miss the self in the
pursuit of hitting the self. Only when one develops
total indifference to the self — which is not a capacity
of the self — is the self's centre hit over and over.

When the self is hit, the student of archery
becomes a Master, and this very transformation
allows him to see that he remains a pupil, a beginner,
and to think of himself otherwise would be folly.
Finally, he sees himself as he truly is, which is to
see nothing at all. This notion immediately struck
me as true. And it has been my life's experience that
on the far side of complexity one only encounters
simplicity: having undergone the training, one finds
oneself untrained.

This experience of becoming a master by discovering one's novicehood was, incidentally, precisely my

---

[1]  Eugen Herrigel, *Zen in the Art of Archery* (London: Penguin
Books, 2004; translation first published 1953), 16.

experience of studying philosophy. When I began my studies as an undergraduate, I felt as if I'd been thrown into a labyrinth of cryptic jargon and esoteric insights, out of which there was no obvious escape. By the end of my degree, however, I had become familiar with what terms denoted which principles, the general assumptions of most important philosophers and their interpreters, and the respective conclusions to which they arrived. Thus, I felt — and this was a feeling confirmed by my receiving the highest award at graduation — that I had mastered the discipline. (Given that most people only undertake bachelor's degrees, this is a state of epistemic illusion in which the majority remain for the rest of their lives, thus one of the tragedies of universalising tertiary education is its acceleration of civilisational decline through the expansion of what some social commentators are calling 'mid-wittery.') On embarking on post-graduate research, however, I discovered that what I had learned as an undergrad was the content of a set curriculum, and in fact I didn't really know anything at all. By the time, then, I received the highest award for my master's degree, I was beginning to intuit the depth of my witlessness. Eventually, I undertook doctoral research under the supervision of two very great philosophers, and my thesis was examined by two other very great philosophers. And having passed with flying colours, I finally had the confidence to assert my utter ignorance.

With Socrates, I can say that the only difference between my present self and my younger undergraduate self is that I now possess certainty about my ignorance, whereas before I just suspected it. Unfortunately, declaring one's ignorance is not conducive to employment in the academy. Universities are packed with fakes who purport to be experts, and they are terrified that the secret might get out that there is no such thing as an expert. In turn, the fakes expect you to do the decent thing and keep up the fakery on which they all depend: pretending to belong to an intellectual elite only works if everyone plays along. Going about asserting that you're not wise at all (but only a mere lover of wisdom) might mean game-over for everyone—and thus will only bring you hemlock.

No doubt Professor Herrigel, the first Westerner to hold a chair in philosophy at a Japanese university, was well aware that his academic discipline necessarily led to Socratic ignorance. And every philosopher must decide whether he is going to be honest about his status as an accomplished ignoramus or become a fake with the rest of them; the former requires the humility to see yourself as you really are. Cultivating such humility is a struggle for the best of us, and the best of us are not found among intellectuals. Thus, to be free to say the truth—beginning with the truth about oneself—one must locate the target: the *self*.

Like Herrigel, I began to practice philosophy because I thought it might be a path to mysticism, and certainly Lady Sophia—as she did Boethius, by her rebukes—has shown me the threshold of her province, the Cloud of Unknowing, beyond which only prayer is of use. Like Virgil outside at the gates of paradise, she has left me there to await my Beatrice. And again, like Herrigel, I did not expect Beatrice to come in the form of Diana, with a strung bow and full quiver.

For six years Herrigel studied archery under Awa Kenzō, a Zen Master and teacher of Kyūdō (Japanese archery). Whilst there, Herrigel was enamoured by the cultural confidence of the Japanese, and regrettably on his return to Germany mistook the Nazi ascendency for the German counterpart of such confidence, becoming a committed member of Hitler's party and wrecking his scholarly credibility in the process. Still, his book on archery remains a spiritual classic that has consequently never gone out of print.

The major theme of *Zen in the Art of Archery*, that archery is not about hitting the target but hitting oneself, is a lesson to which I have time and again returned. As it happens, this is the hidden lesson in all physical education in the West too. The reason the gymnasium has been an essential part of the academy ever since Plato founded it, is because physical activity generates the interior disposition of humility by presenting us with our current limitations, forcing us to depend on others, and providing a vision of the aptitude we'll likely never achieve. Indeed, any displays of humility in the heat of the game we have always been content simply to call 'sportsmanship.'

Archery, however, differs from many other sports in that — outside tournaments — the only person one is playing against is oneself. And because archery is not just a sport but also a martial art, one is more *fighting* oneself than playing against oneself (at least that is how it feels). The main enemy one is fighting, in fact, is the horde of distractions that comes when one wishes to loose the arrow. These distractions drive you to calculate the weight of the arrow against your draw length, to remember the bow's poundage, and to gauge the distance of the target; and they cause you to look down the arrow with one eye closed to estimate how far from the centre you must *aim* in order to hit it. This, for the traditional archer, is all a mistake: his task is to banish that host of rationalisms and 'clear his mind.'

Here I should explain something to the uninitiated. When I speak of archery, I am speaking

of *traditional* archery. (I am a traditionalist in all
things, and archery is no exception.) With an Olym-
pic recurve bow or a compound bow, with all their
weights and sights and balancers and triggers and
levers and pullies and clickers, numerous calculations are required. This kind of archery, however, is closer to rifle shooting than to anything
our ancestors understood by the term. Certainly,
modern archery has its merits, especially in the
bowhunting world, where a clean kill ought to be
one's primary concern. But it's not what I mean by
archery. What *I* mean by 'archery' is the shooting
of wooden arrows with feather fletchings from a
string tied to a wooden stick. To become proficient
at such a simple activity, one must free oneself of
all calculations, and instead just *feel* the shot. In
fact, the traditional archer does not even 'aim' at
the target, but merely 'points' at it, keeping both
eyes open, looking not down the arrow but straight
at the place he wishes to hit. Traditional archery
is not like shooting a rifle; it's much more like
throwing a stone.

A sharp-shooting archer attacking his enemy
was not making mathematical calculations, nor
was a hunter-gatherer who was creeping with his
bow through the undergrowth. Such people simply
looked at their target and shot it. This is even more
obvious with horse archery—a remarkable skill that
is now being revived in Hungary—for which the
calculating brain is of little use, and feelings and
instinct are everything. If one sixteenth-century
woodcut is to be believed, the shooting of fowl from
horseback with a bow was an Imperial pastime
(practised by Emperor Maximilian I, depicted in
the image to which I refer), and such shots could
only have been taken by putting aside calculations
and simply *feeling*, *pointing*, and *loosing*.

Leonhard Beck, *The Prince at the Bird-Catching*, 1514/16

The notion that one will only hit the target when one stops aiming at it—and starts clearing the mind, pointing the arrow and loosing it—is also an important feature of *Zen in the Art of Archery*. As Herrigel argues, one does not even loose the arrow at all; *It* looses the arrow, and only by letting *It* loose the arrow is the arrow sure to pierce one*self*. And *It* is whatever is left when the illusion of *self* has been overcome.[2] Reading Herrigel's book was my first encounter with Zen. Five years later I had my second encounter.

Aged nineteen, I ascended a mountain in Kerala, south India, to join a small community that had gathered around a Jesuit priest whom his followers claimed was *enlightened*—and he had a certificate from Japan to prove it. I stayed for a week, which sufficed to judge that his disciples were unhinged and unpleasant, but it also allowed me six hours of silent 'meditation' per day for eight days, and this taught me something. In this religious tradition, which is certainly not Catholic Christianity, 'meditation' denotes the emptying of one's mind from all distractions in order to remain in a state of mental silence. When, later, I became a Roman Catholic, I discovered that prolonged periods of prayer required a very similar discipline, and, whilst such Christian exercises are undertaken not to empty the mind but to fill it with the transformative presence of God, one must still do battle with the very same enemy: distractions.

That swarm of mental flies torments the devoted hours of the toxophilite too, especially when he seeks to encounter the mystical presence of God in that silent eternity that subsists between loosing his arrow and its penetrating of the target. Archery,

[2] Ibid., 73-74.

therefore, requires deliberate and concentrated rec-
ollection before it can be practiced successfully. And
in the execution of this interior quietening, the
distinction between archery and spirituality becomes
blurred. In the words of Herrigel:

> In order to slip the more easily into the
> process of drawing the bow and loosing the
> shot, the archer, kneeling to one side and
> beginning to concentrate, rises to his feet,
> ceremoniously steps up to the target and,
> with a deep obeisance, offers the bow and
> arrow like consecrated gifts, then nocks the
> arrow, raises the bow, draws it and waits in
> an attitude of supreme spiritual alertness.
> After the lightning release of the arrow and
> the tension, the archer remains in the pos-
> ture adopted immediately following the shot
> until, after slowly expelling his breath, he
> is forced to draw air again. Then only does
> he let his arms sink, bows to the target and,
> if he has no more shots to discharge, steps
> quietly into the background.[3]

Herrigel is describing here a series of acts that border on the liturgical, in which the archer offers
himself and his weapon as "consecrated gifts," and
proceeds to adopt an "attitude of supreme spiritual
alertness," which in fact is realised only in the
self-forgetfulness that comes by concentration on
the task at hand.

Whatever the errors contained in the Zen conception of selfhood, which I'm confident are many, there
remains a truth therein that I think is unassailable.
This is a truth about *ourselves* that is supported by
the classical ethics of the Greeks and the Roman
stoics, and that was purified and transformed by

---

[3] Ibid., 56–57.

Christianity: interior liberty comes by the quad-
ripartite sequence of mastering oneself, forgetting
oneself, gifting oneself, and embracing Reality. What
these terms mean differs according to the tradition
in which they're entertained, but the assumption
from which they spring is the same, namely that we
remain shackled so long as we are preoccupied with
the self, which is the ultimate state of illusion. To
be free to embrace Reality, the self must be hit and
killed — only then can it be resurrected.

Archery, the Japanese have long believed, sup-
plements this interior journey towards a state of
wisdom, a journey that to some degree we must
all undertake if we are to avoid tormenting others
with our unsettled lives. And it is for others that,
in the attainment of wisdom, we discover we exist.
In hitting the self, we hit the target, and from
wherever the self is hit we can pour out ourselves
for the felicity of others. Self-gift and union with
Reality, which I judge to be two aspects of the same
condition, *is* wisdom, and how archery can lead to
its enjoyment will be my final consideration on the
topic of archery.

### III: ARCHERY AS WISDOM

Since the so-called Enlightenment, the West
has been plagued by an obsession with abstractions, privileging them over realities, an epistemo-
logical sickness that has been broadly diagnosed
as Rationalism. Thus, we privilege the so-called
'hard sciences' and mathematics, and we conflate
the *quantifiable* with the *true*, but we stand perplexed
by all that unveils meaning, like art, and culture,
and the disciplines of understanding (rather than
'facts'). Moreover, our preoccupation with abstractions has arisen symbiotically with the 'turn to the
subject' — that is, the turn to the *self* — in a diabolical

concoction of syrupy solipsism, whose ingestion has wholly inebriated the Occident.

As I reflected above, the self is perhaps the greatest illusion. Roger Scruton once remarked to me that, "if one is tempted to turn back to oneself, to encounter oneself, one immediately discovers that there's actually nothing there." When he said this, it filled me with horror. But in fact, he meant that in the attempt to encounter oneself, one must epistemically isolate oneself, but the isolated self is an illusion, given that *I* am only *I* inasmuch as I am *I*-in-relation-to-*You*.

Ideas sundered from the reality from which they're abstracted, especially those that orbit the chief fiction of the 'authentic self,' are at the very zenith of self-deception. Our declining civilisation is one that is in the grip of this illusory condition, which is accordingly expressed by every duped modern, from the teenager routinely taking 'selfies' to the trans-activist who declares his 'true identity' and consequently forces others to say things that both he and they know to be untrue. All such people run roughshod over reality in pursuit of the 'authentic self'—and it's obvious to any sane onlooker that, of course, there's actually nothing there.

The perennial teaching of all wisdom traditions—one that was raised to the status of holiness by Christianity—is that self-actualization comes by self-forgetting and not by self-discovery. And the perfect overturning of this humanising truth by modernity is the ultimate proof both of our epoch's falsity and malevolence. All this stupidity and chaos is derived from starting one's intellectual quest from the wrong point of departure: with the illusion of the self rather than—like a child pointing and asking "what's that?"—with the (much more interesting) world out there. The person, of course, who gave this error philosophical respectability was Descartes, by whom we continue to be cursed.

The reason why, so often in my writing, I advocate hiking, riding, hunting, and foraging, and why I encourage the learning of *real* things, from the history of nations to the names of trees, is because I think we're all very unwell and such things are part of my cure. Now, I want to add archery to this list of treatments.

In *Toxophilus*, by the Tudor-age scholar Roger Ascham, the titular 'Lover of the Bow' addresses his interlocutor with the following words:

> He that would know perfectly the wind and weather, must put differences betwixt times. For diversity of time causeth diversity of weather, as in the whole year; spring time, summer, fall of leaf, and winter: likewise in one day, morning, noontide, afternoon, and eventide, both alter the weather, and change a man's bow with the strength of man also. And to know that this is so, is enough for a shooter and artillery, and not to search the cause why it should be so: which belongeth to a learned man and philosophy. In considering the time of year, a wise archer will follow a good shipman.

Ascham is saying, in sum, that the archer is concerned with the real and the concrete, for it is reality that will affect his shooting, not his ideas about it. The archer, if he is to shoot well, must not mechanically repeat exactly the same motions over and over — as is so often supposed — but must adapt himself to the conditions in which he finds himself, all of which will change him as an archer. Knowing the causes of the effects that affect the archer is the domain of philosophy, as Toxophilus says, but all (good) philosophy begins with *experience* of reality, and such experience is the fundamental prerequisite for good archery.

To put this analysis of archery into the idiom of Iain McGilchrist, traditional archery requires intense *right-brain activity*. Modern archery — with its use of weights and stabilisers, string-walking measurements and sights, etc. — depends on two things: accurate calculations and repetition of the same technique. This entails that perfection in archery is contingent on the degree to which the archer himself can approximate something mechanical. Modern archery, then, is rather a left-brain affair. Traditional archery, on the other hand, depends on sensitivity to conditions, instinct and intuition, and *feeling the shot*. In traditional archery, the calculating brain that reduces reality to computations and abstract categories must become the mere servant — the 'emissary' — of our ability to touch the interconnectedness of things.

McGilchrist has speculated that we may be undergoing civilisational decline, since our current societies are characterised by the typical left-brain dominance traceable — according to his account — in the collapse of all civilisations. He was once asked what our societies would look like if they were characterised by right-brain dominance, to which he replied, "beautifully balanced." And this, it seems to me, is what the archer is seeking, or should be seeking, for himself: to be interiorly, beautifully balanced. He practices archery because he wants to habituate that condition and thereby make it a second nature. Indeed, such an interior state is arguably a precondition for wisdom.

What is perhaps most striking about traditional archery is that it took full advantage of technological developments whilst remaining exactly the same: the bow has changed extensively, but the nature of traditional archery as a sport and a martial art has not. The original English longbow, for example, was simply a single piece of yew wood, cut from the tree where the heartwood (the central part) and the sapwood (the outer part) meet. The shaft was then seasoned for a few years before being slowly worked into shape. The final bow stave had a D cross-section, making it extremely springy. Whatever people mean by a longbow today, however, they don't mean that.

From the eighteenth century onwards, longbows were made from other woods, often imported from America. Bowyers used powerful adhesives to laminate various woods together, adopting techniques that had been used in the Middle and Far East for over a millennium, making the longbow more consistent, perform better, and keep a 'lifespan' of a few more years. Georgians and Victorians added leather or felt handles to their longbows, and beautiful deer-horn nocks at the ends of the limbs.

In 1930s America, an experiment was carried out to reveal the best cross-sectional shape for a bow limb. This experiment was done, in fact, to explain why the English longbow's D-section was superior to all other bow designs. Instead, it revealed that the best cross-section was that of a flat limb. This research finding was then applied to the English longbow. The result was a far more efficient and stable longbow with flat limbs, which could be made from more common woods, with a much longer life (about eighty years, rather than the six years of a modern English longbow), especially if made with added fiberglass. This bow, called the American longbow, has been further developed since, with additions like a shooting shelf (reducing the degree to which the arrow must flex around the bow) and 'reflex-deflex' limbs (on 'hybrid longbows'), making these bows considerably faster.

In each age, the latest technology has been fully embraced to make longbows of better quality, as well as creatively develop other traditional bows such as field-recurves and Hungarian and Ottoman horse bows. Thus, traditional archery is not an antiquarian pursuit, but disturbingly modern. Nonetheless, the *art* of traditional archery has remained unchanged. It is still as simple as a man with a stick and string, shooting wooden arrows. To do this successfully, he must do nothing different to that of the medieval longbowman hunting boar with a stave of yew wood: *clear his mind, feel the shot, point,* and *loose the arrow.*

Archery of this kind returns one to reality — to the concrete, the real, the conditioned. From the spectral web of unanchored ideas one tumbles, landing on a range with the breeze on one's face, bow in hand, staring at a target — missing which might mean a broken arrow. Habituating flights back to reality is an absolute imperative for those who are intellectually inclined. In a breath-taking passage, Roger Scruton reflects on this imperative, and his fulfilment of it through foxhunting:

> Abstract thinkers must renew their awareness of the really real. They should hunger for the sight and smell and touch of things, and nothing brings the sensuous reality into focus more clearly than hunting. This 'Being' that Heidegger refers to, as though it were some glutinous stuff from which the little shoots of '*Dasein*' (you and me) sprout up like curious protozoa — what has it to do with the spring of turf, the ooze of river bank and the muddy grind of gravel in which this sure believing hoof is planted? The ground is not one but many — hard and soft, sharp and yielding, dry and wet, grass-canopied or

raw beneath the scattered rout of last year's
vegetation. Pad, hoof and foot follow in turn
through this multifaceted terrain, grasping
it as an infant grasps its mother, knowing
the taste and touch of every part. And aloft
among these flying animals you re-enter the
state which our ancestors renounced for
comfort's sake.[4]

It is necessary for a philosopher deliberately to
seek out means to free himself from his preoccupation with abstractions. What is courageous,
however, is the choice to return to his philosophis-
ing specifically in order to privilege realities over
abstractions in his thinking (and an exemplary
philosopher in this regard was indeed Scruton). I
use the word 'courageous,' because in so doing the
philosopher declares that his ideas are not reality (as
many philosophers purport of their schemas), but a
mere means to grasp better the reality to which we
are *all* privy. And if his ideas fail to illumine what
we all already know (but perhaps didn't know that
we knew), then such a declaration is an invitation
for us to discard his ideas as vicious snares. Such
an approach entails that he, a philosopher, belongs
to no special class of 'perfecti' or cognoscenti, but
is a man stumbling in the dark just like everyone
else—he just has slightly sharper eyes.

Such privileging of things over concepts by a
philosopher implies that if you travel with him to
the far side of his philosophy, there you will find
nothing other than the world apprehended by the
man on the street, only better lit by the lamps of
thorough thought. Indeed, if you do not find yourself next to the man on the street, then you have
fallen into the hands not of a philosopher at all, but

---

4  Scruton, *On Hunting*, 70-71.

of one of the many evil sorcerers who fill modern humanities departments. And given that evil is not creative, but a privation, you will not only have lost your hold on reality but found yourself trapped in the grey, boring limbo of an 'intellectual system.' And that, I submit, is an interior condition that is perfectly antithetical to wisdom.

Archery is an activity practiced for its own sake. Nonetheless, archery is also, I have been at pains to convey, a *means*—far from the only means, but one that is special to me—to recapture reality as well as the wonder that is the appropriate response to reality. After all, the world we inhabit is an icon of God, testifying both to His beauty and His goodness, as St Thomas Aquinas remarks in the *Summa Contra Gentiles*:

> God, through his providence, orders all things to the divine goodness, as to an end; not, of course, in such a way that something adds to his goodness by means of things that are made, but, rather, that the likeness of his goodness, as much as possible, is impressed on things. However, since every created substance must fall short of the perfection of divine goodness, in order that the likeness of divine goodness might be more perfectly communicated to things, it was necessary for there to be a diversity of things, so that what could not be perfectly represented by one thing might be, in more perfect fashion, represented by a variety of things in different ways. [5]

What Aquinas is saying is that the glorious world around us is itself the communication of God. This is an elementary truth that is impossible to

[5] Thomas Aquinas, *Summa Contra Gentiles*, III, 69, no. 1.

acknowledge for those locked up in the prison of the *self*. The mindless adolescent engaged in habitual selfie-taking—blind to how boring is the idiot on his iPhone at whom he pouts, who in turn pouts back at him, whose vacuity no number of filters will mask— simply cannot see the glorious world around him.

An obligation looms over us throughout our lives, namely to hit the target by hitting the *self*, and only then can we begin to see reality as it is, beginning with ourselves. I have suggested that the practice of archery may be one way to do this. Roger Ascham saw the art of the bow as an essential accompaniment to his intellectual endeavours in the service of our Western civilisation. As the inestimable Samuel Johnson remarks in his biography of Ascham:

> [He] sufficiently vindicated archery as an innocent, salutary, useful, and liberal diversion; and if his precepts are of no great use, he has only shown, by one example among many, how little the hand can derive from the mind, how little intelligence can conduce to dexterity. In every art, practice is much ... precept can, at most, but warn against error; it can never bestow excellence. [6]

As Johnson notes, Ascham's intellect was great, but that very greatness meant little when it came it conquering the art of archery. Indeed, he practiced archery, we might say, to teach himself that despite his great mind, it took only a stick and string to humble him. But by a life spent on the range, with longbow in hand, in the pursuit of excellence in the art of archery, at the end of his life Ascham was able to hit his target.

---

[6] Samuel Johnson, "The Life of Ascham," ed. Jack Lynch, originally printed in *The Works of Samuel Johnson* (1825), https://jacklynch.net/Texts/ascham.html.

Ascham also hit the target in the deeper sense, for he identified the only thing that really mattered. It is recorded that on his life's eve, he thusly expressed his deepest longing: "I want to die and be with Christ." With these words, Ascham departed this world. And since the ancients whom Ascham so carefully studied believed that you could judge a man's life by the way he died, we can assume that his many accumulated hours of loosing arrows were pregnant with his profoundest longing, namely for union with the Saviour. This, I judge, is wisdom.

AFTERWORD:

# THE HUNT
# FOR LEADERSHIP

## BY CHARLES COULOMBE

FOLLOWING HIS 2023 BOOK *CON-servatism and Grace*, the author of this volume of meditations is better known as a political philosopher of establishmentarian, traditionalist conservatism than an outdoorsman.[1] Those who know him personally, however, know that he would far rather discuss hunting and conservation than anything else. Indeed, just as it was for his teacher Sir Roger Scruton, so it is for Dr Morello that conservatism and conservationism are two sides of the same coin, so to speak. In this book, however, he has offered us a refreshingly unpolitical series of meditations, and whilst he may be always keen to indicate the moral and social ramifications of his insights on hunting and outdoorsmanship, he clearly privileges the spiritual significance of his pursuits above anything political. I wish, therefore, to take it upon myself to offer as a closing thought a reflection on hunting as an education in genuine leadership, even statesmanship.

Most people today would agree that many of our problems stem from a lack of decent leadership. It has occurred to me that one of the reasons for this is symbolised by a feast day in early November—that of St Hubert, patron of hunters. Having

---

[1] See Sebastian Morello, *Conservatism and Grace: The Conservative Case for Religion by Establishment* (London: Routledge, 2023).

pursued a stag on Good Friday, the sixth-century Frankish nobleman was surprised when the stag turned to face him, a crucifix appeared between its antlers, and his quondam quarry warned him to follow Christ if he wished to escape the fires of hell. Becoming a monk, he evangelized the Ardennes where formerly he had hunted — and ended as Bishop of Liège. Little-known in most of the United States, devotion of St Hubert is a big thing in Central Europe, as well as France, Belgium, and most of the Mother Continent. Key to the celebration of St Hubert's feast day is Holy Mass featuring music provided by hunting horns (a bit jarring, but quite pre-Vatican II), followed by the blessing of the hounds. Whether used in packs to chase deer, fox, or boar, or singly to pursue smaller game, dogs are of course a key part of the hunt.

In the Western mind, the hunt is a part of the mystique of the forest, which plays for the European — either in his home continent or in the diaspora — the same role that the desert, jungle, or the islands of the open sea play in the cultural minds of the other peoples of the Earth. From the depths of that forest that is at once mystery, sustainer, and opponent, our ancestors found simultaneous food and shelter and the need to defend themselves against enemies, real or imaginary. The hunt was a key part of this landscape of the imagination.

Even those Englishmen and Central Europeans who have never hunted for game outside a restaurant menu may wear tweeds or *Trachten*; no hotel or eatery can claim to be truly 'rustic' without antlers hanging around. Orbiting the hunt itself — whether with horse and hounds, deer stalking, or pheasant shooting — has grown up a whole body of customs and folklore. Devotion to St Hubert, the sound of the horn signalling various occurrences in the hunt,

the jargon called 'Hunter's Latin' in German, and
customs such as 'blooding' new hunters (smearing
some of the vanquished animal's blood on the first-
timer's cheeks) are just some of these.

Of course, in today's ever increasingly confused
mental climate, hunting is under attack as never
before. The same disordered mentality that has
difficulties with gender distinctions also has difficulties distinguishing between species. Having
ceased to believe in God, the West has ceased to
believe that man has any particular prerogatives
as His noblest creation. Part of this is veiled in
supposed concern for the environment. One must
say "supposed," because the truth is that hunters
have always been the greatest conservationists, for
obvious reasons. If all the hiding places of the
quarry are destroyed and the game itself hunted to
extinction, there is no more hunt. Thus, from early
on, hunting larger game was reserved to Europe's
royalty and nobility. As a result, most of the more
venerable national parks and forests that dot the
Mother Continent began as game preserves, even
as such noted castles and palaces as Windsor and
the Louvre started life as hunting lodges (the latter particularly reserved for wolf-hunting, hence
the odd name). Certainly the most noted hunting
museums in Europe tend to be in such buildings,
ranging from France's Chateau de Chambord to
Germany's Schloss Kranichstein.

Indeed, hunting and its mystique became an inte-
gral part of kingship. As the historian Murray
Pittock has written: "The Stuarts made much of
hunting: it helped to confirm their heroic status as
stewards of nature and the land. In doing this, they
identified themselves not only with Arthur, but
with Fionn, the legendary Gaelic warlord who was
in the eighteenth century to be the subject of James

Macpherson's pro-Stuart Ossian poems."[2] The same has been true of most of Europe's dynasties down to the present; according to *The Royal Encyclopaedia*, "Despite protests by anti-hunting groups, the Prince of Wales takes a close interest in the sport at all levels and has defended it as an effective form of sporting conservation of wildlife and its habitat in the British countryside."[3] Indeed, there was a great deal of mewling in the press when HRH 'blooded' Prince William on a deer stalk in the Scottish Highlands. But the same practices are followed by the Kings and Queens of Benelux, Scandinavia, and Spain; King Juan Carlos in particular routinely faced criticism for his love of hunting.

An unpleasant truth is that much of the hatred of hunting with hounds—whether fox, hare, or deer—has its roots in class envy. Animal rights activist, vegetarian, and National Socialist dictator Adolf Hitler banned it in Germany in 1934, extending the measure to Austria in 1938 (alongside the ban on home-education, this piece of Nazi heritage has been lovingly maintained by subsequent governments in both countries). Socialist Tony Blair honoured the 70th anniversary of Hitler's achievement with a similar law banning the hunting of live quarry with hounds in Great Britain, and six years later Nicolas Sarkozy ended the French Presidential Hunts. The media of course lauded all of this as progressive—a fact that by itself should be enough to make us question the prudence of it.

I myself have not hunted for any game in decades save what can be found in restaurants, by which point it is customarily already dead. But I do not

---

[2] Murray G.H. Pittock, *The Invention of Scotland* (London: Routledge, 2016; originally published in 1991), 4–5.
[3] *The Royal Encyclopaedia*, ed. Ronald Allison and Susan Riddell (London: Macmillan, 1991), 271.

approve of the fashionable limitations placed on
hunting; in fact I cannot really trust any leader
who does *not* hunt. It would be much better if they
all did. My reasons are not merely for tradition's
sake, nor for historical parallel. Nonetheless, there
*are* obvious tactical advantages to rulers hunting
together; consider, for example, the meeting of
Maximilian, Sigismund of Poland, and Wladislav
of Hungary and Bohemia at Wiener Neustadt in
1515; the hunt at Skierniewice, Poland in 1884, at
which Emperors Alexander III of Russia, Wilhelm
I of Germany, and Franz Josef of Austria-Hungary
were present; and Franz Josef and Tsar Alexander's
son, Nicholas II, at Mürzsteg in 1903: all hunt meet-
ings where important policy decisions were made
between various Monarchs and other rulers. This
is no accident. The qualities that the hunt forces
us to cultivate are those that I, at least, would like
to see in modern rulers.

The first is perhaps obvious: the hunter must
display courage. Whether hunting on horseback or
tracking a wild boar through foliage on foot, he
puts his life, his health, or, at the very least, his
comfort at risk. There are, of course, other ways to
do this — one might serve in a war, for example —
but for most, hunting is the most accessible. Why
is this important? National leaders often demand
that young folk in the military or police risk their
lives in performance of their duty. What better way
to understand exactly what one is asking of one's
citizens than to put one's own precious life on the
line occasionally?

Secondly, the hunter must develop his intelli-
gence. The quarry is canny and determined, driven
by nature to preserve its own life. The sort of silly
thinking that characterizes our current overlords'
efforts in their elevated posts simply won't work in

the field. One must learn the habits of the prey and use well-cultivated reason to apply one's learning to particular cases. And the hunt is unforgiving ... for the hunter is either triumphant or he is not; all the verbiage in the world cannot cover up failure for the hunter who returns empty-handed.

The hunt also requires a certain amount of physical fitness — decidedly a good quality for those in leadership. Depending on the kind of hunting, the sport may require profound organizational abilities and high executive function. One may have to evaluate the real talents of hounds, horses, and men according to a real and objective standard, and one will need to deploy those talents in a prudent, decisive way to succeed. There is no room for maundering on the field! In the moment of pursuit, mere ideology or connections cannot replace the discerning of real ability.

In a word, hunting over forest and field forces a man or woman to deal with a terrible truth: there is an immobile and unmalleable reality to which each of us must accommodate ourselves to accomplish what we want to achieve. All the bloviation in the world shall alter that reality not one iota. One may throw the latest theory at the countryside, or cite as many politicized 'scientific' studies as one wishes; the countryside simply smirks back, and the quarry vanishes into the implacable forest.

The leader who encounters objective reality during the hunt may go on to make all sorts of other discoveries: that all of life is gendered in only two sexes; that over-expenditure of time and energy leads to loss; that all things die; and much else of similar importance. This may, in time, bring other realisations to Their Excellencies. In place of mere 'environment' — a mostly notional thing made up primarily of statistics, used to advance a progressivist agenda—there is a splendid reality called 'nature.' Rather than being a mere political convenience, nature is something to which, in some manner, all of us must accommodate ourselves.

Beyond nature, our hunting leaders might well discover that on which all nature is contingent, namely God. They may not be struck down by a vision as St Hubert was, but no one who develops a close comradeship with nature can fail to see that there is a design in nature, and that things really do fit together well. This, in turn, might lead to a sense of duty towards the plot of ground they course over; towards the county, province, and country in which it is situated; towards their fellow humans who share that land; and perhaps even to that God Who made it all and ever holds it all in being. There are few so patriotic as the regular hunter—and few who are so faithful.

It was said earlier that I was not going to justify having our leaders hunt by recourse to the past, and indeed I shall not; but it is nevertheless enlightening to look at a few of the leaders whom the hunt produced. Blessed Emperor Charles I of Austria was devoted to the hunt (although his great uncle, Emperor Franz Josef, and his uncle, Archduke Franz Ferdinand, were far more proficient in their pursuit of quarry) and he proposed to his future Empress Queen, Servant of God Zita, at a hunting lodge. Victor Emmanuel III of Italy was a tireless follower of the chase; no doubt this lent him at least some part of the moral fortitude necessary to depose Mussolini and the Fascists in 1943. Although one may well debate the final outcome of Juan Carlos's facing down an attempted coup in 1980 and some of his later actions, no one can deny his physical courage. So it goes with innumerable monarchs.

But what of elected officials? Theodore Roosevelt was one of the United States' most remarkable presidents, and whatever one thinks of his legacy, we cannot deny that he was a champion conservationist. His love of sporting pursuits was unambiguous:

> In hunting, the finding and killing of the game is after all but a part of the whole. The free, self-reliant, adventurous life, with its rugged and stalwart democracy; the wild surroundings, the grand beauty of the scenery, the chance to study the ways and habits of the woodland creatures—all these unite to give to the career of the wilderness hunter its peculiar charm. The chase is among the best of all national pastimes; it cultivates that vigorous manliness for the lack of which in a nation, as in an individual, the possession of no other qualities can possibly atone.[4]

Charles de Gaulle was an avid hunter as well as the creator of Free France; he declared that "War is like hunting, except that in war the rabbits shoot." Churchill approvingly cited an opinion of one of R.S. Surtees' fictional foxhunters: "Mr. Jorrocks has described fox hunting as providing all the glory of war with only thirty-five percent of its danger." So it goes. A huge proportion of the world's best leaders have been hunters; the fact that so few of our overlords do so today does not reflect well on the present crop of potentates.

I use the word "overlords" deliberately, because I cannot well describe today's heads of state as "leaders." Their incompetence in general; their fecklessness and fear expressed in despotism; their moral

---

4 Theodore Roosevelt, *The Wilderness Hunter: An account of the big game of the United States and its chase with horse, hound, and rifle* (New York: G.P. Putnam's Sons, 1893), vii.

turpitude—all this indicates their remoteness from reality. Perhaps hunting should be made a requirement of selection to office.

Let us not forget that before his conversion to the religious life by the miraculous stag with the crucifix between its antlers (think of the Jägermeister logo), St Hubert was Master of the Household to Blessed Charlemagne's great-grandfather. His mystical hunting ground was today's massive Ardennes Forest; the proximity to this beautiful area, rich in game, led Charlemagne to create his capital at Aix-la-Chapelle, Aachen. So, while we should pray for hunters and hunted alike each year on the feast of St Hubert—whether or not we hear the hunting horns at Holy Mass, or see our dogs blessed—let us also pray for the rulers and the ruled. Perhaps, then, our relationship shall once again be more like monarch and subject than pursuer and prey.

www.ingramcontent.com/pod-product-compliance
Lightning Source LLC
Chambersburg PA
CBHW031431270326
41930CB00007B/659